Baptist Ecclesiology

Matthew Walker

Published by Trust House Publishers

ISBN 978-1-945774-55-3

Typesetting services by BOOKOW.COM

To Vernon Rooney and Ricky Knox
and their wives GayNell and Ellen Jane—the first
deacons at College Park
Baptist Church.

Foreword

Having been reared as a pastors kid, I've been around church all of my 52 years. During my personal ministry experience of pastoring for 30 years, I've been eyewitness to the theology, philosophy, and practice of hundreds of churches in multiple denominations. I'm so thankful for the faithfulness and clear testimony of so many of the local fellowships with which I've interacted.

Having observed and served in these local churches, I can confidently say a review of their ecclesiology at least once every generation would be a healthy practice.

Matt Walker's work provides just that; a theological, philosophical, and practical review of a Bible centered, local church's ecclesiology only in a modern-day context.

We all know how easy it is for our churches to merely go through the motions of "doing church" in any given generation. But Matt's book provides your assembly in our time a spiritually healthy approach to a sound ecclesiology. It will aid your fellowship's ability to self-evaluate the health and existence of your local body.

As shepherds, staying on mission is what we desire. Having known Matt for 30 years, I can tell you he knows what it means to stay on mission. You can tell by the passion with which he writes. He's very interested in helping churches maintain sound, local church doctrine that leads to underpinning a clear, concise, and compelling pursuit of Great Commission living in our church and local communities.

You and your flock would do well to study this volume at this time for the eternal benefit of the souls of this generation under your care and in your personal Jerusalem.

Tim Potter | Senior Pastor | Grace Church of Mentor, Ohio

Preface

I love the church. I get to spend nearly every day in an office beside the place where I preach on Sundays. Like other pastors, I get tired—ministry life can wear you down quickly. But there is a spring in my step almost every day as I walk across our parking lot and unlock the door to my study. The room is filled with memories. There are pictures and poems on the walls and a couple large bookcases which hold well-worn copies of commentaries that I either purchased, or rescued when other people were throwing them away. I love books. My Marine Corps dress blues are on a mannequin over by the window, a sentry to guard against anyone who would dare to steal something from my desk.

My desk is my dad's that he gave me when he retired from his pastorate. It was built for him by Earl Nutz, a retired Bible professor at Bob Jones University. I love the desk even though I cannot get one of the drawers open. It's the perfect desk for a pastor. Out the back window from my office is an old barn. Our church property used to be a tobacco farm, and I hope I never forget how God provided it to us when it looked like we would be in rented facilities forever. I often hear church members fire up the lawn mower in that barn before they begin mowing the 4 acres surrounding our facility. I love hearing that sound—the noise of God's people doing his work.

I love the trees on the church property. When the town of Cary, NC gave us the permits to build our church building, it included the requirement to plant over 700 trees and shrubs. The cost was so overwhelming that our church family determined to plant them ourselves. For three weeks in the Fall of 2011 I watched people give up their Saturdays (even in pouring rain) to plant those trees. I developed more than one blister digging holes in Carolina clay.

I love my secretary. I should mention that my wife Becky fills that role. Not many people get to work with their spouse, but it is privilege that I enjoy every day. I watch her care for the church as much as I do and sometimes think that God can give women a pastor's heart even if they don't serve him in that office. I love that my own children grew up under my ministry. I have hundreds of little memories of them as they matured in Christ. I love the deacons and other church leaders who serve at College Park. They are some of God's finest servants. We have not always agreed, but we have nearly always agreed to be agreeable, something many churches do not experience. I love the members of the church. They have forgiven me a thousand times over for all of the stupid, ignorant, immature things I've said and done over the years. They have willingly submitted themselves to my leadership. One of my favorite times of the week is standing out beside the front door of the church and greeting them as they come to worship. I love the children of our church. I love interacting with them as their spiritual shepherd. I learn their names, and I enjoy watching them learn God's word under my ministry.

Most of all, I love standing behind the "sacred desk," opening up God's word, and teaching people who are eager to hear what God has revealed about himself in those holy pages.

I love the church. It's a dear and precious thing to me. I hope you learn to love it as much as I do.

Matthew Walker
Pastor, College Park Baptist Church
Cary, NC

Endorsements

At a time when our civilization is being submerged into eclecticism, secular subjectivity, and therapeutic deism, God's calendar moves on toward the destiny He has ordained. The vehicle that God has established to implement His divine plan on earth is the Church. In a biblically authentic and spiritually empowering presentation Dr. Matt Walker has invited us to understand the Church and thus shine the light of the glory of God through the Church. A remarkable feature of this work is that every section flows naturally from the author's experience in a Christian home and in a Bible-preaching church. Each analysis then is anchored in sound biblical hermeneutics.

Dr. Walker's study of Baptist Ecclesiology is thorough, balanced, clear, and authentic, and practical. Each aspect of the doctrine is presented in its totality, including definitions, biblical teaching, examples, and application. This book can be a vital source of inspiration, instruction, edification, guidance, information, and encouragement to every church member, pastor, Sunday School teacher, college professor, and seminary student. I highly recommend it as a college or seminary textbook, training manual, and personal devotional guide.

Barkev S. Trachian, Ph.D.
Piedmont International University

It has been a joy to observe the life and ministry of Dr. Matthew Walker over many years. His life is a great blessing to me personally. You will find his writing to be thought-provoking and challenging. His words are clear and direct. He brings much experience and education to his presentation. How good that he has taken time to help the gospel cause in this way.

Bruce McAllister, D.Min.
Gospel Fellowship Association

Matthew Walker is well-qualified to write this book on the church. He pastors a thriving church which, with the Lord's help, he planted several years ago.

Dr. Walker is also well trained as a theologian. I'll not recite his academic "pedigree" here, but he is an intelligent brother in Christ, and well educated.

This study of the church reflects excellent research in God's Word. It also reflects Pastor Walker's love for Christ and for the people to whom he ministers at the College Park Baptist Church. I'm grateful for his ministry, his shepherd's heart, and his friendship.

Fred Moritz, D.Min.
Former Director, Baptist World Mission

Contents

Chapter 1

What is a Church?

THERE is a fun little trick that children learn where both hands are pressed together with the index fingers extended upward. A short poem follows that goes something like this: "Here is the church, and here is the steeple. Open the doors and see all the people." Usually, you wiggle your fingers around to make it look like there are people inside your clasped hands.

This whole rhyme begs a question: "Can something be called a church just because of its building, its doors, its steeple?" Throughout church history, the word *church* has often been used in reference to a building.[1] For instance, Notre Dame which burned in April 2019, is considered a church even though its main contribution is in its architecture. Is physical structure what constitutes a church?

Consider the "churches" that are part of a group known as Sunday Assembly. According to the Sunday Assembly website, this group has seventy chapters in eight countries with more than 3,500 attending. The people gather to sing songs, hear inspirational messages, and form a community together. It does not self-describe as Christian, and it is not even very religious. The Sunday Assembly was formed by two British comedians who wanted something like church but "totally secular and inclusive of all—no matter what they believed."[2]

Sunday Assembly is part of the rise of the so-called secular "church" which does what churches do but without any god. These secular

---

[1] Millard Erickson, *Christian Theology*, 1037.
[2] https://www.sundayassembly.com/story, accessed February 8, 2019.

"church-goers" reject the supernatural.[3] Dr. Phil Zuckerman, professor of sociology and secular studies at Pitzer College in Claremont, California, recognizes these people as those who want a "belonging component" without a belief in a god or the supernatural.[4] Sunday Assembly is not located in Europe only. There is a Sunday Assembly in Chapel Hill, North Carolina. Their speaker in early February 2019, Dauv Evans, spoke on his journey *out* of faith.[5]

Can Sunday Assembly be called a church? They sing songs. They meet as a community. They even claim a three-phrase slogan that sounds "spiritual": *live better, help often, wonder more.* Does all of this make them a church? The biblical answer is "no." That leads us to another but more important question. If a group of people who gather together around a particular set of beliefs is not a church, then what *is* a church?

Definition

Some scholars define a church as "the people of God, the assembly and body of Christ, and the fellowship of the Holy Spirit."[6] Others argue that a church is a people who are bought by the blood of Jesus. Further, a church is "the only God-appointed institution authorized to carry out His program of witness and service on earth during the present age."[7] When the Bible refers to a church, these concepts are generally in view.[8]

The Greek word *ekklesia* is very important to our understanding of the doctrine of the church.[9] Native Greek speakers used the term prior to the New Testament era to refer to a gathering of people in a political

---

[3] Leon Neal. https://www.theweek.co.uk/93733/what-are-atheist-churches, accessed February 8, 2019,.

[4] Ibid.

[5] https://sundayassemblychapelhill.org/, accessed February 8, 2019.

[6] Edmund Clowney. *The Church: Contours of Christian Theology*, 28.

[7] Rolland McCune, *A Systematic Theology*, III: 195.

[8] Our word *church* is derived from the Greek *kuriakos* which means that which belongs to the Lord. See Millard Erickson, *Christian Theology*, 1041.

[9] The Hebrew words *qahal* and *'edah* are Old Testament terms that refer to a congregation of people.

sense.[10] The town crier would call the citizens of a town to assemble.[11] The purpose of the assembly was democratic self-governance "for the discussion and decision of public business."[12] And Luke uses the word in that way in Acts 19:32 to refer to the near riot in Ephesus. The people gathered in response to the silversmith's concern about the impact of Paul's preaching against their idol-making business. This assembly was an *ekklesia*.

The writers of the New Testament used this word *ekklesia* to define the nature of the church. This actually changed the meaning of the term. Instead of referring to democratic self-governance in a Greek city-state, *ekklesia* came to mean an assembly of *Christians*.[13] "Here was a new kind of *ekklesia*—a Christian *ekklesia*—and it was distinct from every other *ekklesia* because it had the message which Jesus Christ gave it."[14] In a non-technical sense, *ekklesia* meant a physical unity of people. The Christian influence on the term shifted that meaning slightly so that *ekklesia* technically means not just physical unity, but also spiritual unity. Thus, as Charles Ryrie puts it, the best way to think of the church is not as being called out, but rather "called-together."[15] *Jesus calls the church together to both physical and spiritual union. Ekklesia* must mean both locative presence (in the same place) and theological unity. Both ideas must be maintained.

With this in mind, the church is "a unified people of God (location) that have been saved by grace through faith in the sacrificial death of Jesus Christ, baptized by the Holy Spirit, submissive to the biblical requirements of church leadership and function (doctrine), and called-together for the purpose of accomplishing God's mission on earth during this time (dispensation) for His glory (dedication)."[16] The four

---

[10] Charles Ryrie, *Basic Theology*, 393.

[11] Not every citizen was part of the assembly. In the Greek city-state, those who were part of the *ekklesia* were men who were older than 18 years of age. See "Ecclesia: ancient Greek assembly," *Encyclopedia Britannica*, https://www.britannica.com/topic/Ecclesia-ancient-Greek-assembly, accessed March 5, 2019.

[12] Earl Radmacher. *The Nature of the Church*, 122.

[13] Earl Radmacher. *The Nature of the Church*, 131.

[14] Earl Radmacher. *The Nature of the Church*, 130.

[15] Charles Ryrie, *Basic Theology*, 394.

[16] This definition is used to apply specifically to local churches.

parenthetical terms—location, doctrine, dispensation, and dedication —explain the meaning of the word *church*. Any group of people, however well-intended, that does not meet these criteria are not a church.

What About the Universal Church?

There are more than one-hundred uses of the word *ekklesia* in the New Testament, the majority of which refer to a local assembly of Christians.[17] In a few instances, however, the word is used in reference to all believers from Pentecost to the Rapture of the Church (dispensation). "The universal church represents the aggregate, not of local churches, but of believers in the Lord Jesus."[18] One example of this kind of usage of *ekklesia* is Matthew 16:17, where Jesus promises to build his church. This promise is not to build a singular local church, but to build *one* Church. Another example is in Ephesians 3:21, where Paul ends his doxology by exclaiming that God should be glorified in the church by Christ Jesus for all eternity. The meaning of this use of *ekklesia* includes both churches in Paul's day and every church up to the present. Furthermore, it must extend out into eternity. "Since there will be no local church in any meaningful biblical sense in heaven, it is difficult to see how this usage can refer to the local church."[19]

Some pastors and Bible teachers object to the term "universal" church while admitting that there must be a record of those who are believers in the Church Age for all time—those who are part of local churches on earth combined with those who are already in heaven with Christ. Some substitute phrases like "family of God" or "people of God" while maintaining a distinction between Israel and the Church. Dr. Rolland McCune from Detroit Baptist Theological Seminary explained the difference between local churches and the universal church using the phrase "the body of Christ" as a distinguishing mark. He

---

[17] Charles T. Grant, "The Nature of the Universal Church," *Emmaus Journal*, EMJ 07:1 (Summer 1998), 6.

[18] Ibid, 6.

[19] Rolland McCune, *A Systematic Theology of Biblical Christianity*, (Detroit: Detroit Baptist Theological Seminary, 2010), 3: 210.

argued that the body of Christ is "the whole spiritual body of true Christian believers of this age regardless of location or circumstances. It is the total number of Spirit-baptized believers ... whether they are in heaven or on earth."[20] However, McCune agreed that any concept of a universal church did not have any structure or leadership that possessed authority over others within the local church. He wrote: "The Body of Christ in itself has no organization and no function on earth except as expressed in local churches."[21]

I think that the universal sense of the church is best understood within the context of the eschaton. The few references to the church being universal looks forward to the time when everyone who is saved during the Church Age will be gathered together into one church. In that context, there is no universal church today, but there will be a universal church in the end times when every believer joins in unison proclaiming the glory of Jesus Christ. This is when there will be the church united. There is a church universal, but it is in the future, not something that is in place today.

Keeping that in mind, the best way to understand the word *ekklesia* is that it primarily refers to local churches and that the structure and design of the church in the New Testament is explaining how Christians should gather together in individual locations. The rest of this book is about the local church.

Two Theological Considerations

Differences in Minor Doctrines. Some churches disagree with one another over non-essential doctrines. That disagreement does not make one group a church and the other a non-church. For example, there are differences between Baptist/Bible churches and Methodist and Presbyterian churches. This definition of the church does not mean that *only* Baptists can constitute a church and that Bible churches are outside that definition. Differences in church leadership and function,

---

[20] Ibid. 201.
[21] Ibid, 207.

though sometimes very radical, do not mean that one is a church and the other is not. As of this writing, there are some fine Bible churches that adhere to the essential, core doctrines of the Bible. There are also Baptist churches that do not.[22] The definition of "church" does not require complete doctrinal uniformity but agreement on the core doctrines of the faith. We should interact with these churches with both grace and peace.

Israel is not the Old Testament Church. One of the most difficult aspects of theology is understanding the relationship between Old Testament Israel and the New Testament church.[23] There are some, particularly in Covenant Theology, who argue that Israel has been replaced by the church and read back into the Old Testament the concept of the church.[24] Flip that around, and some dispensational theologians argue that there is no relationship at all between Israel and the church. Some dispensationalists go further and argue that the Old Testament has *no* value in the life of a New Testament believer. This position is labeled hyper-dispensationalism.

There are some areas of overlap between Israel and the church (think: same God, same Messiah, relationship to the New Covenant) and areas of distinction.[25] Some of the key differences include the Old Testament land promises of the Abrahamic and Davidic covenants, the ministry of the Holy Spirit in the lives of Old Testament believers versus His ministry today, the perspective on Jesus (Old Testament saints looking forward and New Testament saints looking back), and specific eschatological concerns. For any struggling to see the difference between the two, a good rule of interpretation is to think of how the original text was received by its original audience. An example is the interpretation of 2 Chronicles 7:14 where God promises to "heal the land" of the Israelites if they repent of their wickedness against him.

---

[22] The point here is that denominational distinctives are not the issue. The issue is whether a church is adhering to the core doctrines (orthodoxy) of the faith. Additionally, there may be differences in or concerns about practice (orthopraxy) and even the affections (orthopathy).

[23] See *Continuity and Discontinuity: Perspectives on the Relationship Between the Old and New Testaments*, ed. by John S. Feinberg.

[24] See Arnold Fruchtenbaum, *Israelology*, 680.

[25] See John S. Feinberg, *Continuity and Discontinuity: Perspectives on the Relationship between the Old and New Testaments.* (Wheaton, IL: Crossway), 1988.

This is not a promise of revival to Christians living today. It actually is a promise rooted in God's words in Deuteronomy.

Two Contemporary Applications

Right Doctrine but Lacking Components. Christian institutions (like a Bible college) that gather for a worship service on Sunday morning are not "having church." The believers in attendance are likely members of a local church that meets in another location, and they are church members in the general or *universal* sense, but the service itself is not the same as being in a church. In a Christian college worship service, there is physical unity, but some aspects of spiritual unity are lacking. The gospel may be preached, but the preacher is not necessarily a biblical pastor (according to biblical qualifications). There are no deacons. There are no ordinances observed (baptism and communion). No church discipline is enacted even though campus discipline may be administered during the week by school leaders. Such organizations are generally considered to be "para-church." They organize and operate outside the normal parameters of what constitutes a biblical church. These organizations often provide great benefits to local churches, and the people within these organizations are typically members of a church, but the organizations themselves cannot be considered to be churches.[26] (One helpful thing to keep in mind is that it is unfair to apply church standards to a Christian college or organization. They cannot be considered a non-church on the one hand and then be expected to maintain church standards on the other.)

False Doctrine. Likewise, a group of people who gather around a set of beliefs that are contradictory to *core* New Testament doctrines cannot be considered a church. Core doctrines include the gospel, and the other theologies such as Christology and Soteriology (doctrine of

---

[26] Mission boards, Bible Colleges, and Christian camps are examples of para-church ministries. Likewise, there are Christian charities that are parachurch that emphasize some aspect of helping people in need. Many of these are good ministries and nothing should be inferred from what is written here that they are not appreciated for their work.

salvation). There should be some flexibility to allow for minor differing interpretations, but a denial of Christ or the gospel is a nonstarter. There is no atheist "church" because atheism argues the exact opposite of the Bible. Mormonism is a cult, not a church. The Jehovah's Witnesses have a building that they call their "church," but their meetings do not constitute what the Bible defines as a church because they teach doctrines (particularly about Jesus) that are essentially anti-Christ. They deny His deity. This is also why Sunday Assembly cannot be considered a church: Its members deny the fundamental truth that God exists.

A New Testament Example: The Church in Thessalonica

The church in Thessalonica is a perfect example of a church as defined by the Bible. The first verse, 1 Thessalonians 1:1, reveals that Paul's intended audience was the church (*ekklesia*) in Thessalonica. This greeting to the Thessalonian believers implies a sense of physical unity—they were designated by their location. But this opening chapter of Paul's letter also emphasizes spiritual union in God. They were saved by the gospel of Jesus (v. 5). The result was that they became disciples of Paul and his ministry team (v. 6). They even had some kind of interdependence with churches in Judea who were suffering the same kinds of persecution from the Jews that the Thessalonian believers were suffering at the hands of their own countrymen (2:14).

Paul also points to three specific evidences of the Thessalonians' salvation. Specifically, he commends them for their work of faith, labor of love, and patience of hope (v. 3). Their work of faith was evident as they "turned to God from idols to serve the living and true God" (v. 9). The key terms in verse 9 are *turn* and *serve*. The phrase "turned to God" is likely a reference to repentance, the kind of turning from sin to Christ that is necessary for conversion. Paul uses similar language in his testimony before Herod Agrippa, claiming that God sent him to preach the gospel to the Gentiles so that they would turn from darkness to the light (Acts 26:17-18). It is also important that even as they turned from idols, they turned to serve God. This is the word commonly used for slavery in the ancient world. It recognizes submission to God as the only one worthy of worship.

Paul also commends them for their patience (endurance). This hope was evident as they waited for the return of Jesus, the "Son from heaven" (v. 10). The doctrine of salvation does not just entail rescue from sin, but includes a transition from the kingdom of darkness to the kingdom of Christ. The Thessalonian believers were being persecuted, but they had hope in Christ's return that enabled them to endure their trials gladly.

Finally, their labor of love was evident in the report from Timothy, who recounted to Paul not only the soundness of their doctrine, but also the warmth of their love (3:6). It is easier to see love than faith. Faith is usually internal, the beliefs that motivate people to action. Love is also internal, but the evidences of love are usually external. Timothy's report included the fact that the Thessalonians were eager to see Paul and the rest of his ministry team. They also loved each other, something that Jesus indicated was a mark of discipleship. "By this will all men know that you are my disciples, if you have love for each other" (Jn 13:35). In fact, Paul reveals that this love was something God Himself had taught them (4:9).

This *ekklesia* in Thessalonica gathered together in one place because of mutual relationship to God and each other by the gospel of Jesus. They were indwelled by the Holy Spirit (1:5-6). Paul encourages them to submit to the biblical requirements of church leadership and function (5:12-13, 27). Some other aspects of God's mission through the church on the earth are also mentioned concerning this group (5:14-22). And the result was that even though this church was relatively new, they became an example to others (1:7-8) at that time and are still a good example to us.

Discussion Questions

1. Are you part of a local church? Why or why not?

2. Does your church meet the four concepts (location, doctrine, dispensation, dedication) that define a church? Why or why not?

3. Do you think it is okay that Christians gather for worship services that are not part of a local church? Explain your answer.

4. Do you think your church is like (or striving to be like) the one in Thessalonica? Why or why not?

Chapter 2

An Emphasis on Gathering

WHEN I began writing this book in June 2019, I had no idea how important the doctrine of church (ecclesiology) would prove to be in 2020. Coronavirus, and the government's response to the pandemic, tested churches unlike any time in American history. In North Carolina, my home state, the governor used his emergency powers to shut down every kind of gathering including church services. For a few months, we held virtual services on YouTube and sermonaudio.com because that was all we were legally allowed to do. After some of those restrictions loosened, our church began holding services outside. We moved indoors in early Summer as the outdoor temperatures climbed into the low 90's.

I remember the joy I felt the first Sunday morning when many in the church returned to worship together in-person. This experience taught me that the biblical emphasis on gathering together is not just a good idea but a mandate from the Lord. A church is not just people who are in spiritual unity by the gospel. As the definition of the term "church" in chapter 1 put it: "a church is a unified people of God (location) ...." The Greek word ekklesia implies a physical unity alongside a spiritual one. In that chapter I cited Charles Ryrie's helpful interpretation that ekklesia means "called-together."[1] As we met under the pine trees on our church property, I remembered various times in Church History when God's people were forced to gather in less than ideal

---

[1] Charles Ryrie, *Basic Theology*, 394.

conditions. I remember a famous painting of a Russian church gathered in the woods on a cold, snowy Sunday morning because it there was no free church in the Soviet Union. I also remembered reading of the great black preachers in the American South prior to the Civil War who led their congregations in worship while hiding in the forests because it was illegal for them to assemble. Many of them suffered incredible hardships for their faith, particularly because of their belief in the importance of a church gathering together.

Gathering in the Early Church

I also remembered that believers in the Early Church were often forced to gather in secret locations because of localized persecution by Rome. In comparison to our present experience, first century believers did not have very much. They did not have Bibles like we have today. There were no Bible colleges and seminaries, missions agencies, Christian camps, or religious-based charities. They simply did not exist at the time. They also did not have church buildings like we have. However, the lack of formal space did not prevent them from gathering together. Christians met in homes.[2] The apostle Paul refers to this arrangement in at least one location when he mentions the church that met in Philemon's house (Phm. 2).

First century Christians were identified by their connection to their local church. It was the center of their spiritual identity. Consider Acts 2:46. "And they, continuing daily with one accord in the temple, and breaking bread from house to house...." There was no spiritual identity as a follower of Jesus that did not include a tangible connection to a church. Today's Christian insult "Bible-thumper" would have been something like "church-goer" in the Early Church. Those who assemble together in a church service on Sunday are publicly identifying with

---

[2] The early church probably followed the Jewish model of having a synagogue when the opportunity to build such facilities became available. The word *synagogue* is a derivative of two words. *Syn* is a Greek preposition meaning "together," and *agein* means "bring." The synagogue was where the Jewish people were brought together. We have an English word for that in Christianity: It's called a church.

that church just by being there. It is a "unified people of God (location) …."

This unity might be tested by reality when the congregation is pressured by external dangers such as war and disease like the coronavirus, and by internal conflict, or even heresy. Yet, it is the unity of a body of believers that, in part, defines the church. For example, the church in Corinth was fractured by internal divisions (1:10) over class and church politics, but Paul still referred to them as "the church of God which is at Corinth" (1 Cor. 1:2).[3] While they were struggling to remain unified, there was a sense in which they were united. They still gathered together as a church.

This is also evident in the way Paul writes to the Corinthian believers. He refers to things that were "among you" (*en humin*). These things are revealed in the *seventeen times* this phrase "among you" is used in 1 Corinthians.[4] The apostle considered them to be one church that gathered together.

Most obvious is how this is used in 1 Corinthians 5 where Paul scolds the church for its willingness to continue fellowship with a church member who was living in gross sin (5:1): He was "among" them (vv. 1-2), Paul says. The apostle identified that the inclusion of this man was a serious problem and tells the Corinthians that when they "gathered together" (*sunago*), they were to deliver up this individual to Satan (v. 5). His sin was dangerously infectious like a little leaven (yeast) that eventually spreads through an entire piece of dough, leavening the whole lump (v. 6).[5] This individual had to be cut off from the rest, an action that would only be possible if "the rest" was an identifiable unit.

---

[3] It is a bit ironic that the church singled out in the Bible for disunity is also the church where the idea of uniting together is most discussed.

[4] 1:6 (the testimony of Christ was confirmed "in you") 1:10 (that there be no divisions "among you"), 1:11 (there are contentions "among you"), 2:2 (not to know anything "among you" save Jesus Christ….) 3:3 (there are "among you" envyings, and strife, and divisions….) 3:16 (the Spirit of God dwells "in you"), 3:18 (if any man "among you" seems to be wise….) 5:1 (there is fornication "among you"), 6:2 (if the world will be judged "by you"….) 6:5 (is there not a wise man "among you?"), 6:19 (the Holy Spirit is "in you"), 11:13 (judge "among yourselves"), 11:18 (there are divisions "among you"), 11:19 (there are heresies "among you"), 11:30 (many are weak and sickly "among you"), 14:25 (God is "in you"), 15:12 (how say some "among you").

[5] This passage will be reconsidered in chapter 9 on the subject of mutual accountability.

The consequence of Paul's language is one very important idea: In order to be a church, *there must be assembly*. If a group is incapable of assembling, it may function in other ways like a church and even confess a doctrinal statement faithful to Scripture, but it violates this one fundamental ideal. If the church in Corinth could "come together" (*synerchomai*), it stands to reason that this is one of the things that constitutes a church.[6]

Reasons Why Gathering Is So Important

The gathering of believers together is important for at least three reasons. First, it is important because assembly reflects our eternal state. The apostle Paul pleaded with the Thessalonians (2 Thess. 2:1-2) not to be easily troubled because the day of Jesus was imminent, and he encourages them by writing that their *gathering together* with Jesus would be very soon (see comments in chapter 1 on the Universal Church). The wording in verse 1 is the same idea used when we talk about a church gathering together on Sunday. The *physical* gathering together of believers in the local church reflects the kind of being together that we will experience in the future in heaven as a Universal Church. When a church today joins in song worshipping Jesus, there is a brief hint of eternity in the room. Someday the congregation of the redeemed will sing with one voice praises to the Lamb who was once slain but is risen and alive forevermore.

Second, assembly is important because this is one of the means by which believers encourage each other in the Lord. The writer of Hebrews encourages Christians to be active in provoking other believers to both love and good works (Heb. 10:24-25). This is part of the "one-anothering" that is necessary for the New Testament church (see chapter 8). This is only accomplished by the means of two important qualities. First, the provocation to love and good works is to be performed when the church gathers together. Christians should not forsake the importance of assembly. While Christians can encourage others online, over

---

[6] The subjunctive verb *synerchomai* is modified by the word *holos* which is translated "whole." The *holos ekklesia*—whole church—came together.

the phone, and in other settings, the main idea of the New Testament is that this encouragement is to be done in person at meetings of the church. Instead of forsaking the assembly, Christians gather in order to exhort each other with a sense of urgency—the day of Christ is approaching.

Finally, assembly is important because the body of Christ functions as a body when the church gathers together. Paul told the Ephesians that the body of Christ is "fitly joined together" just like a human body is joined and connected. Each body part is put perfectly in place in order that together all the parts can effectually work in unity for the sake of the whole (Eph. 4:16). The entire concept of spiritual gifts is based upon the assumption of assembly. The body is one, Paul writes, even though it is composed of many members (1 Cor. 12:12). Using the human body as a metaphor, every church has feet, ears, eyes, and a nose (vv. 15-17). Likewise, the church has members who fulfill very specific roles in order to help the church function as it should. If the body parts are cut off from each other, then the body cannot function as it should. Without assembly, it just does not function properly.

Modern Approaches That Deemphasize Assembly

With the combination of technology and an increasingly post-Christian society, some churches are adopting new approaches to the way to "do church." While the motive for these new approaches may be pure (for example, a desire to reach people for Christ or an effort to find a better way to "do church" in our culture), many of them undermine the gathering together of believers. For example, there is an approach called "digital church" where people "assemble" online instead of in person.[7] For a few months in early Spring 2020, nearly all of the churches in the world adopted the "digital" approach. There are some obvious problems with this method. How can anyone determine who is actually "present" in such a church? How does this church accomplish the various tasks a church is biblically supposed to do? How

---

[7] Thom Rainer, https://thomrainer.com/2014/02/six-major-issues-regarding-the-digital-church/, accessed March 11, 2019.

does such a church distinguish between believers and unbelievers? At the present time, there are no good answers to these questions. In a country closed to the gospel, such an approach may be necessary for safety's sake. However, most Western-world Christians are not in a situation where gathering together is inherently dangerous.[8]

Another new approach to church is the multi-site model. In this approach, a church is divided across a region in different locations. Each local assembly has its own "on-site" pastor (and possibly on-site staff). Each separate site typically has its own live music. What joins the sites together is a common preacher whose sermon is broadcast on a screen. Leaders of such churches argue that "the essence of a local church is a covenant body, not a manner of assembly."[9] The tangible connection, they say, is doctrinal, not physical: "To say that 'assembly' means all people in one place at one time is suggestive at best."[10] They also say that the argument that a church must assemble as one group automatically rejects the multi-service model (a church having more than one service on a Sunday). And they argue as well that church historians do not believe that the Jerusalem church could have assembled all in one place.[11]

The problem with these arguments for the multi-site church model is that they are not derived from the Bible, but from philosophical and pragmatic bases. As the earlier portion of this chapter indicates, physical assembly *is important* in the life of a church. Furthermore, using a questionable model that many have adopted (multi-service) as a defense of another questionable model (multi-site) is really not a very strong argument. Finally, while it may be difficult to determine how churches met together in the early days of church history, this cannot

---

[8] This approach is not inherently wrong. For example, it would have been helpful if such technology existed during the time before the American Civil War. Many godly people were forced to assemble in secret because they were slaves and meeting together was outlawed. See William L. Andrews, *North Carolina Slave Narratives: The Lives of Moses Roper, Lunsford Lane, Moses Grandy, and Thomas Jones* (University of North Carolina Press, 2003).

[9] J.D. Greear. https://jdgreear.com/blog/why-the-multi-site-strategy-is-biblical-and-can-be-the-wisest-course-of-action-for-a-congregation/, accessed March 11, 2019.

[10] Ibid.

[11] Ibid.

be used as a proof-positive argument in favor of deemphasizing assembly. (See a helpful response to these issues in one pastor's outline of twenty-two concerns about the multi-site model.[12])

Discussion Questions

1. How do you think Christians should respond to a situation like a pandemic (or a war)? At what point do you think governmental laws should be ignored as obedience to Christ?

2. The second reason why churches must gather together is for mutual encouragement among believers. How does your church encourage this?

3. What happens when the church rejects gathering together? Consider the third reason why Christians should gather in church.

4. How does the multi-site or multi-service model of church threaten the requirement to gather together?

---

[12] Jonathan Leeman. https://www.9marks.org/article/twenty-two-problems-with-multi-site-churches/, accessed March 11, 2019.

Chapter 3

A Sacred Atmosphere

IMAGINE Moses standing in Horeb, in a remote part of the desert.[1] He is surrounded by flocks of sheep and goats belonging to his father-in-law Jethro. There is nothing particularly special about the ground in this area. The weather in that region ranges from warm to very hot depending on the time of year. The environment is desert scrub and dirt. The kinds of animals in Jethro's flock are notoriously smelly. Shepherding a flock like Moses is doing is hard work.

Now, imagine him looking over the sheep and goats and seeing a bush in the distance—on fire, but not burning up (Ex. 3:2). Moses sees that sight and moves toward it to investigate how such a thing could be happening. As he turns toward the bush, God calls to him. He tells Moses to stop moving toward the bush and take off his sandals (v. 5). The reason God gives for this command is straightforward: "The place where you stand is holy ground."

Consider the context of Moses hearing God's statement. Moments before, maybe less than an hour earlier, these animals were probably nipping at this specific bush, trampling the ground around it with their hooves, and doing all the sorts of animal things you would expect from a herd of sheep and goats. Yet now, Moses is required to stand back and remove his shoes, something that his culture demanded when in the presence of God.[2] So, before God arrives on the scene, the bush

---

[1] Walter Kaiser, Jr. refers to this area as the Valley of er-Raha. See "Exodus," in The Expositor's Bible Commentary, ed. Frank Gaebelein, (Grand Rapids: Zondervan, 1984), 2: 315.

[2] Cameron Kippen, "History of Sandals," accessed March 18, 2019, http://historyofsandals.blogspot.com/2010/10/egyptian-sandals_22.html.

and ground around it are just like any other common place. After God arrives, the entire area becomes consecrated, set apart.

The biblical principle is that any space where God is *automatically* becomes holy ground. This is so important for our understanding of church worship that it is difficult to overstate. The space God occupies is holy. The space may have been previously common, possibly even corrupt, before God's presence *fundamentally* alters that place. Think about this: Because God promises to be present wherever His people gather, church gathering places are consecrated (Matt. 18:20).

This transformation is possibly most evident in church planting where a church may gather in non-church-like facilities.[3] What was a barber shop on Saturday may be holy ground on Sunday. What was the mall's food court during the week is God's space on Sunday if a church is meeting there. The furniture store, bank building, funeral home, and even an auditorium of a false religion[4] could be immediately transformed by the presence of God.

What makes a place holy is not the atmosphere created by the architecture, by the stained glass, or by the acoustical effect of the auditorium. Many buildings have one or all of these qualities, but lack the most essential ingredient—the presence of God. Holiness is not a contrived effect. Holiness does not necessarily "feel" holy. And at times, we use this word inaccurately. For example, a place is not holy because the area is the site of some great event or is a place where many lives were lost. There is nothing holy about the battlefield in Gettysburg, Pennsylvania, even though many died there during the Civil

---

[3] Our church began in a hotel. The first "nursery" was just a common hotel room. Typically, the night before we rented the room it was occupied by others. Whatever occurred in that room was common and possibly profane. After a good cleaning up by the hotel staff, the room was converted to a nursery facility for the purpose of watching small children while their parents attended church. The space of the hotel that the church rented for worship was a common meeting room. Monday through Saturday, companies and organizations used the space for common purposes, to conduct business. On Sunday, that space was transformed into a church as God's people gathered together for worship. What was common was changed into something sacred. People were spiritually saved from sin in that room. Others were changed by God's Spirit in that room. For those few hours on Sundays, that space was consecrated ground.

[4] A church plant in Queens, NY uses the building of a Christian Science "church." For a couple of hours on Sunday morning, the building houses Satan's people. By early afternoon, the building becomes a place of true worship where God is exalted. It becomes "holy ground."

War. Cemeteries, such as Arlington National Cemetery, are solemn reminders of the price of our freedom , but they are not truly holy ground, at least not from a biblical perspective. They may be solemn places, but it is best not to confuse solemnity with holiness. What makes a place holy is that *God is present.*[5]

A church signals one of its chief purposes in gathering together to meet with God and to worship Him. When the church meets, the location where it meets must be considered consecrated. As long as God's people are meeting there for the purpose of worshipping Him, it is a place consecrated to Him. Anything set apart to God is holy. It is sacred.

Ways to Categorize Things

There are three ways to think about the nature of things around us. They can be consecrated—set apart to God, common—have nothing to do directly with God and thus be morally neutral, or corrupt—something that violates God's moral or ethical code. It is pretty obvious that Christians should be involved in consecrated things, and maybe involved in common things, but should have nothing to do with corrupt things. These categories provide a helpful means for testing the way a church should function in relation to its culture.

Consecrated

Consecration is the idea of declaring something to be sacred, set apart to God.[6] It involves a sense of holiness and purity. The term, *sacred,* is from the Indo-European "sak," derived from Latin *sacer,* meaning holy or dedicated.[7] There are many English words that begin with the four letters *sacr* that are derived from this root, such as sacrilege, sacrifice, and sacrosanct. The Oxford Dictionary defines sacred as "connected

---

[5] There is a difference between God's omnipresence and the presence of God.

[6] Merriam-Webster Dictionary, https://www.merriam-webster.com/dictionary/consecrate, accessed May 10, 2019.

[7] "Sacred," American Heritage Dictionary, accessed February 11, 2019, https://www.ahdictionary.com/word/indoeurop.html#IR094600.

with God or a god or dedicated to a religious purpose and so deserving veneration."[8] Some of the synonyms of the word offer a fuller look at its meaning: cherished, revered, religious, blessed, consecrated, divine, and solemn.[9] Likewise, some of the antonyms of sacred, such as blasphemous, irreverent, dishonorable, and cursed, provide a well-rounded understanding of our English definition of sacred.[10]

Sacred also has a linguistic connection with the Old Testament term holy (*qadash*) and its New Testament equivalent (*hagios*).[11] In the Old Testament, sacred things where those that were set apart to God, hallowed to Him, consecrated. A general scan of the numerous verses using this term reveals that it could refer to an individual like a priest, or a special place such as the tabernacle or the temple, or a special day or assembly. In the New Testament, sacred or consecrated is used in a more ethical sense to denote separation from worldliness. Of course, in both Testaments the most common usage is in reference to God, though less so in the New Testament.[12]

Christians are expected to be consecrated to God (Rom. 12:1). Everything having to do with God or the Christian life is expected to be consecrated to Him, to be sacred. If something is used for God's work it must be considered consecrated.

Common

Those things which are not set apart to God are considered common or secular. Common things are those items which have no real spiritual significance. There is nothing special about common things. The clothing of Jesus, for example, was not sacred. Some people, particularly those who are caught up in mysticism, try to place significance on

---

[8] "Sacred," Oxford Dictionaries, accessed February 11, 2019, https://en.oxforddictionaries.com/definition/sacred.

[9] "Sacred," Thesaurus.com, accessed February 11, 2019, https://www.thesaurus.com/browse/sacred.

[10] "Sacred," Power Thesaurus, accessed February 11, 2019, https://www.powerthesaurus.org/sacred/antonyms.

[11] See the Septuagint translation of Genesis 2:3 as an example.

[12] "Holiness," International Standard Bible Encyclopedia (Grand Rapids, Eerdmans) Vol. 3, 1404.

relics or other objects. If one could possess a piece of Jesus' cross, for example, that would be a very interesting and important artifact, but it would not be holy. Secular things are the common things of life. They are temporary things that do not have the same value as those that are considered sacred by God. The burning bush was just a shrub, meaningless and unimportant before it began to burn with God's presence.

There is also nothing sinful about common things. Secular does not necessarily mean sinful or worldly. If a lamb was set apart to God as a sacrifice, that lamb was considered holy, and the other lambs of the flock were not holy. Yet the non-chosen lambs were not considered evil. From a personal business perspective, those other non-holy lambs would be considered common.

There is also a sense in which common things of our lives are influenced by God. For example, the Old Testament Jews gave a portion of their crops to the Lord as a tithe. Those offerings were consecrated. They were devoted to the Lord. The rest of their crops, though not strictly sacred, were still governed under Jewish laws. For the Christian today, every part of life should be voluntarily submitted to God's complete control so that while not necessarily sacred, there is still a sense in which our lives are his dominion.[13]

Corrupt

A final category, corrupt things, consists of items considered bad, sinful, or even very profane. In the Old Testament, the word *profane* (*chalal*) refers to things which are polluted and defiled. For example, Reuben corrupted his father's bed by engaging in adultery with Bilhah, Jacob's concubine from Leah. Reuben's sin with Bilhah is an example of something extremely wicked, but God also commanded the Israelites to refrain from using cut rocks to make up His altar (Ex. 20:25). To build the altar with hewed stones would be to profane or corrupt the altar. In the New Testament, the wicked are described as lawless and unholy (*anomos*).

---

[13] Sporting events are a great example of this. Christians often pray before they play sports for God's blessing and protection, but the game is not sacred. It is not evil either. It is common.

The Church Is Consecrated

In 1 Corinthians 3, the apostle Paul asks the believers in Corinth if they were aware that their church was a temple of the Lord (v. 16). Using the word temple (*naos*), Paul draws their attention to the Jewish temple in Jerusalem, a location they would have recognized as one of the holiest places on earth. Paul's reason for writing about this is to explain that God's Holy Spirit indwells not only individual believers, but in some manner He also indwells the church as a whole. The Corinthian church was holy to the Lord. Paul uses a play on words to explain how seriously God takes this truth: If any person, he says, defiles (*ptheiro*) God's dwelling place—the church, God will destroy (*ptheiro*) that person.

God's people must consider themselves and their church to be holy before the Lord. This is non-negotiable. Wherever God dwells, that place is holy. Isaac Watts put it this way:

How sweet and aweful is the place
With Christ within the doors,
While everlasting love displays
The choicest of her stores.[14]

Outside the doors of the church, there may be something akin to Sodom and Gomorrah, but "within the doors" is the "sweet and aweful" (modern idea of awesome) place. In this life, God's domain and Satan's may be separated by only a thin piece of glass. But they must remain separated.

In every dispensation, God's people have been called to be holy, to be separate from the world. Israel was called to be different from the nations around them. They were to worship and serve God alone, unlike the pagan nations of the world. They were a kingdom of priests, a holy people, and a light to the Gentiles.[15] But one of the main points of emphasis by the Old Testament prophets is that Israel failed in their task.

---

[14] Isaac Watts, Hymnary.org, accessed March 18, 2019, https://hymnary.org/text/how_sweet_and_aweful_is_the_place.

[15] R. Kent Hughes, *Set Apart: Calling a Worldly Church to a Godly Life* (Wheaton, IL: Crossway), 17-18.

Likewise, the church is a kingdom of priests, a holy people, and a light to the world (1 Pet. 2:4-5). We are to be set apart and called to a life of holiness.[16] The gathering of God's people must be different from other assemblies in the rest of the world. The church must consider its assembly to be a sacred hour. Like Moses at the burning bush, it is no time to be wearing shoes, as it were.[17] The sacred activities of our worship should be performed in a sacred manner with an appropriate spirit.[18]

That Which Corrupts

If asked, "What do you think *corrupts* a church?" most Christians will probably respond by naming some gross sin on the part of its leaders or some evil tolerated by the congregation. There is no doubt that moral sin defiles a church. However, the first warning that Paul gives to the Corinthians is the area of *doctrinal* corruption. He states that as the church planter in Corinth (1 Cor. 3:6), he was working like an architect (v. 10), someone who sketches blueprints of a building. He laid the foundation, which he later identifies as the doctrine of Jesus Christ (v. 11).[19] He also names Apollos, a very influential first-century preacher, as being vital to the spiritual development in Corinth (v. 6). Together, he says, they planted and built up the church in Corinth. After them, others came to build on what these two godly men started.

This is where Paul issues a warning. The present leaders in Corinth were to be cautious in how they built up God's church. They needed to be very selective in the building materials they chose. They could use

---

[16] Ibid, 21.

[17] Kaiser, "Exodus," *The Expositor's Bible Commentary*. 2: 316.

[18] Consider the Ark of the Covenant in Kirjath-Jearim after it had been returned by the Philistines (see 1 Samuel 6). When David took Zion from the Jebusites, he determined to place the Ark in his political capital. He took a large retinue of people with him to bring the Ark to Jerusalem. In the attempt to move the Ark, there was an accident involving the oxen, and Uzzah attempted to steady it, grabbing it with his hands. God killed Uzzah for his act of irreverence (2 Sam. 6:7). God's actions, while seemingly harsh, should be understood in view of God's holiness. As one Old Testament scholar wrote, this story "requires that sacred tasks be done in a sacred manner." Eugene Merrill, "2 Samuel," *The Bible Knowledge Commentary*, Old Testament, 463.

[19] This is probably best understood as the *regula fidea* (rule of faith).

things such as gold, silver, and precious stones or they could settle for wood, hay, and stubble (v. 12). The valuable materials are metaphors for right doctrines: The leaders in Corinth could add to the foundation that Paul had laid and that Apollos had expanded by teaching right doctrines, those in keeping with the teaching of Jesus. But Paul is warning against use of worthless materials—metaphors for bad or false doctrine, which he identifies as that which will corrupt a church.

In chapter 5, Paul explains the more common view of how a church can be corrupted—*moral* corruption. In this chapter, the Corinthian congregation was tolerating the actions of a man who was engaged in horrible sin (1 Cor. 5:1). Moral corruption is just as dirty as doctrinal corruption. Our culture celebrates gross sin—"lewdness, pornography, adultery, sexual violence, sexual humor, and double entendre" are part of the fabric of our society.[20] The consequence of this cultural acceptance is that "both heterosexual and homosexual fornication (a-marital sex) have been declassified from the category of sins."[21] People who engage in such behavior consider themselves to be morally good people.

Specifically, the internet, a major part of the average American's daily life, is the main portal for corruption through pornography. Each day, sixty-eight million internet searches relate specifically to pornography, about twenty-five percent of all searches on the internet.[22] But as stated earlier, the believer's body is sacred to God. It should be considered "a living sacrifice, holy" (Rom. 12:1). Paul reminded the Corinthians that their bodies are temples of God because of the indwelling Holy Spirit (1 Cor. 6:19). When Christians engage in these kinds of behavior, they bring moral corruption into their lives and into the church.

---

[20] Hughes, *Set Apart: Calling a Worldly Church to a Godly Life*, 79.

[21] Ibid.

[22] "Internet Pornography by the Numbers; A Significant Threat to Society," Webroot, accessed April 25, 2019, https://www.webroot.com/us/en/resources/tips-articles/internet-pornography-by-the-numbers.

Consecrated Does Not Mean Formalism

Unfortunately, some believers are unaware of what consecrated means, and the result is that they confuse formalism with holiness. It is true that sacred activities should be approached in a somewhat formal manner. God is not pleased by a flippant attitude as we worship Him. However, there is a difference between approaching God with a sacred spirit and dressing up or acting in a formalistic way. One is a worshipful expression of the heart; the other is just tradition.

Some Christians, and often by extension their churches, make the mistake of thinking that they are not defiling God's sacred space *because* they participate in formalistic traditions. These traditions usually apply to how they present themselves outwardly—how they fix their hair or what they wear, or how they conduct the worship service in church. Neckties and dresses are not sacred. Even worse, these Christians may actually be tolerating doctrinal or moral corruption.

Formalism is not worship, and it does not exalt God. It replaces the right spirit of worship with some manmade cultural standard—usually of a bygone era, just "going through the motions" of so-called worship. Moses took off his sandals because that was his culture's expectation for a worshipful approach to God. But God expected that same spirit in Moses' heart. It was not the act of removing his sandals itself that was honoring to the Lord. It was the heart of submission and obedience that God desired. More information on this subject is provided in Appendix 2.

Take Off Your Shoes

God desires His church to be a consecrated place, not common or corrupt. It is vitally important that believers approach God with this in mind. Elizabeth Barrett Browning wrote about the connection between sensory things (what you can touch) and spiritual things (what you cannot touch) in her poem "Aurora Leigh." Drawing on the idea of our close contact with the sacred, she reminds us, "Earth's crammed with heaven, and every common bush afire with God: but only he who sees, takes off his shoes, the rest sit round it and pluck blackberries."[23] When the church assembles to worship God, it is a sacred time. There should be a holy hush among God's people.

Discipleship Questions

1. Does your church treat worship as sacred? How can you tell?

2. Are there common things, morally neutral things, that a church can do which does not detract from the sacred atmosphere it is trying to create? If so, name some of them.

3. Two corrupting elements presented in the chapter were doctrinal and moral corruption. In what way have you seen this creeping into the church? What can your church do to prevent it from happening?

4. In what way has formalism replaced the goal of being sacred?

---

[23] Elizabeth Barrett Browning, Aurora Leigh, 86. https://www.bartleby.com/236/86.html, accessed May 10, 2019.

Chapter 4

The Elements of Corporate Worship

Tʜɪɴᴋ of yourself as a citizen of Rome living in Turkey, in the region where the Lycus and Meander Rivers meet. You are standing in the courtyard of a large home in Laodicea. The year is AD 59, and the home where you stand as a guest is owned by a wealthy businessman named Philemon.[1] It is Sunday morning, and you are joined there by a large gathering of people who call themselves Christians or "followers of The Way." One of the first things that you notice is that the people in attendance represent a variety of ethnicities and economic backgrounds. It rings strange to your ear, but a household slave addresses the crowd, calling everyone's attention to himself as if he possesses some special authority in the group. He begins with a prayer to God, but not to any of the Roman gods with whom you are familiar. This God is different from all that you know.

After the slave finishes his prayer, he opens a scroll, one that is obviously well-worn with much use. He begins to read from the scroll about the God named Jesus Christ Who offers to these people both grace and peace (Col. 1:2). Furthermore, the man reads about how this Christ has rescued them from Satan's kingdom, redeeming them and forgiving their sins (vv. 13-14). Even more astounding, or at least it seems so to you, this Jesus is said to be the Image of the invisible God and the Creator of all things (vv. 15-16). You are left breathless as the

---

[1] Arthur Rupprecht, "Philemon," *The Expositor's Bible Commentary*, ed. Frank Gaebelein, (Grand Rapids: Zondervan, 1984), 11: 453.

man then states that this Jesus is alive after being dead, something you have always considered to be impossible (v. 16).

After reading for a while, the man begins to expound on the reading. He speaks about the importance of living in a way that would please Jesus by bearing fruit and by increasing in the knowledge of God (v. 10). And though you are unsure what this fruit-bearing is, it seems to have some spiritual meaning. He also states forcefully that Christians are to give thanks to God because of their salvation (v. 11). The man's speech ends with another prayer to Jesus.

Then the people begin to sing:

Jesus, in the form of God,

Did not regard it as robbery to be equal with God,

But He poured out Himself, taking the form of a slave.

Being in the likeness of man,

And being found in likeness of man,

He humbled Himself,

Being obedient unto death, even death on the cross.

Therefore, God has highly exalted Him to the highest place

And given to Him a name that is above all other names,

That at the name of Jesus, every knee should bow—

Both in heaven and earth and even under the earth—

And every tongue should confess that Jesus Christ is Lord

To the glory of God the Father.

After the song ends, several men walk through the group, collecting money, and you are unsure of its intended purpose. A closing prayer is given, and then the adults stand around for a while, talking about the speech and the song, and about more mundane things of life. The children seem a little less interested in conversation and run throughout the crowd, playing some sort of game of chase. An hour or so later, all sit down for a meal together as the conversation continues.

Even though some of the specifics have changed, there is little difference between the way that early Christians met and worshipped in their churches from the way we do today. In fact, with the exception of some of the most recent innovations in church practice, the church of Jesus has been "doing church" nearly the same way for about two thousand years. A first-century church service included all of the same elements of worship that a twenty-first century biblical church has today.

Praying

While much of the biblical data on prayer refers to personal communion between a believer and God, prayer is also an important activity in the life of a church. The New Testament is filled with examples of churches praying together. The church in Jerusalem gathered, waiting for the coming Holy Spirit, and Luke records that they were praying (Acts 1:14). Later, the church came together to pray about the opposition they were experiencing to their mission (4:23-31) and about Peter's imprisonment (12:1-17). The church in Antioch prayed for wisdom (13:1-4). The church in Philippi began because some Jewish proselytes who had not yet heard of salvation through faith in Jesus were meeting for prayer on the banks of a river (16:13-15). The Ephesian pastors met with Paul and prayed together (20:36-38). The church in Tyre met for prayer (21:1-6).[2]

---

[2] See Andy Davis, "Looking to the New Testament for Models of Corporate Prayer," accessed April 29, 2019, https://www.9marks.org/article/looking-to-the-new-testament-for-models-of-corporate-prayer/.

According to this pattern and example, every church meeting should include prayer. For many churches, the worship service begins and ends with prayer. Often, a Sunday service includes a pastoral prayer. Discipleship meetings can include a time of prayer. Men's and women's Bible studies may feature prayer. And the church can also meet for times of special prayer when needs dictate a greater emphasis on praying.[3]

Scripture Reading

Public reading of Scripture is another important feature of a church's worship service. Some churches choose to read portions of the Old Testament and New Testament (particularly the Gospels) every Sunday. The early believers did not have access to a Bible and were dependent on the public reading of Scripture for most of their access to God's divine revelation. Christians today have greater access to God's Word, but this does not minimize the importance of public reading of the Bible.

John Broadus outlines four important concepts regarding public Scripture reading: (1) A devotional text should be selected. (2) The reader should make every effort to read well. (3) Some comments explaining the reading are appropriate. (4) The text that is read should typically be longer than a verse or two.[4]

This provides opportunity for the church to have their minds engaged with God's word before the beginning of the pastor's message. The Bible is a special book and its words interact with the mind in a way that is different from ordinary speech. Churches that avoid reading Scripture are missing out on an opportunity for God's Spirit to work in hearts before the pastor says one word of his sermon.

---

[3] I attended a church service at a mega-church while on vacation in Orlando, Florida. The facilities were well-maintained and the music was choreographed with the preaching. With the exception of a group chant led by an assistant pastor before the offering was taken, there was no prayer at all. The service did not open with prayer, there was no prayer during the middle of the service, and there was no closing prayer. I was shocked. What kind of church calls itself Christian or evangelical and does not pray?

[4] John Broadus, *On the Preparation and Delivery of Sermons*, (San Francisco: HarperSanFrancisco, 1979), 319-20.

Singing

The apostle Paul writes that the Spirit-filled Christian should be in the habit of "singing and making melody in [his] heart to the Lord" (Eph. 5:18-19). Music is a vital part of the worship service. Part of our orthopathy (right affections) is that our spirits or attitudes are aligned with the Holy Spirit. This alignment is often expressed musically as Paul notes in the Ephesians text. Music speaks to the soul. Church music is usually a combination of lyrics and melody. While the words of the poem may speak to the mind, the sounds and rhythms of the music speak to the heart.[5] The combination is emotive. It is a response of worship to God for what He has done for us: Scripturally, it is connected to giving thanks to God (Eph. 5:20).

Because of music's capability to move us powerfully in worship, it is imperative that church music be focused on God and what He has done. Too many Christian songs focus on us—our needs and desires, our experiences, what we think and fear.[6] But church music should be the combination of a text that is biblical with a melody that properly fits the text. Above all, both text and music should be sacred.

Preaching

Paul commanded Timothy to "preach the Word" (2 Tim. 4:2). This has been the pastor's task since the earliest days of the church: He is to "feed the church, the flock of God" (Acts 20:28; 1 Pet. 5:2). The sermon is the central feature of a worship service. It is the public proclamation of God's Word. While there are various methods of preaching, the most useful is the expository approach. Expository preaching is not a style of preaching. Rather, it is an approach to preaching that seeks to draw meaning out of text itself. It is a sermon grounded in the biblical

---

[5] This is what C. S. Lewis called the "chest" in *Abolition of Man* (San Francisco: HarperCollins, 2009). See chapter 1, "Men Without Chests."

[6] See David de Bruyn, quotation of Henry Liddon, *The Conservative Church*, (Religious Affections Ministries, 2016), 77.

text. All of its points arise from truths that are in that text.[7] Its purpose is to proclaim what is in the text, not what one might *think* is there.[8] Its goal is to inform, persuade, convince or convict, and inspire. It is the result of sound exegesis (drawing out), using a literal, grammatical, and historical hermeneutic.

Unfortunately, many pastors do not labor in the Word in order to draw out of it the intended meaning of its human (and divine) author. Instead of practicing exegesis, they perform eisegesis—the exact opposite. Instead of revealing the authorial intent of the text, eisegesis reads into the text the interpreter's biases, presuppositions, and opinions. While it is possible that an eisegetical approach can result in a "biblical" sermon, such an approach is very dangerous. Eisegetical sermons are often more attention-grabbing and thought-provoking, exciting the emotions of the listener. The eisegetical preacher "conjures it all up into an hour's worth of jokes that amuse, pithy sayings that cause a smile, homemade wisdom that draws approving nods, false optimism that elates, moving stories or maudlin tears that stir up people to pity, or passionate cries that provoke extreme emotion."[9] Many in the congregation sing the eisegetical preacher's praises, and he revels in their adulation. However, eisegesis runs the risk of exalting something other than God's truth and thus, cannot produce biblical change.

Giving

The monetary offering collected on Sundays is not part of a church "fundraiser." The pastor(s) or deacon(s) do not plead for people to give so that the church budget can be met. Instead, the offering is a wholly spiritual act where Christians give willingly and cheerfully (2 Cor. 9:7) as God has prospered them (1 Cor. 16:2). Giving is part of worship. And just as there is a solemnity in our approach to the teaching and preaching or God's Word, so there should be an equal concentration

---

[7] See Eric Raymond, "What is Expository Preaching?" accessed April 29, 2019, https://www.thegospelcoalition.org/blogs/erik-raymond/what-is-expository-preaching/.

[8] David Helm, *Expositional Preaching*, (Wheaton, IL: Crossway, 2014), 12.

[9] David de Bruyn, *The Conservative Church*, 51.

of seriousness as we give to the Lord. (More on giving and financial support of the church will be presented in chapter 11.)

Observing Ordinances

The final element of worship in a New Testament church is the observation of the ordinances of Jesus. These do not necessarily occur every Lord's Day as the other aspects of worship do.[10] Historically, churches have observed two ordinances: baptism and communion.[11]

Baptism

Different religious groups have practiced various methods of water baptism. Roman Catholics believe that baptism is a means of grace that "effects a transformation bringing a person from spiritual death to life."[12] Lutherans have a similar belief about baptism but soften the Catholic position by stating that faith is already present in the one being baptized.[13] Presbyterians believe that baptism is the means by which one is brought into the covenant. Many of these believe also that baptism has replaced circumcision as the sign of the covenant, justifying the baptism of babies.

Most baptistic churches hold to a different view of baptism as a public testimony of salvation, a "believer's baptism." It is a water baptism that is representational evidence of what the Spirit has already done in the heart of a believer—washing sins away and bringing one who was spiritually dead to new life in Christ.

The New Testament provides two arguments in favor of believer's baptism over other approaches. First, every instance of baptism in the New Testament involves individuals who had consciously committed

---

[10] Some churches do observe the Lord's Table every Sunday.

[11] Some Christian groups observe a third ordinance, the rite of foot-washing. Baptists generally deny foot-washing as an ordinance for the church because it is not repeated in the Epistles.

[12] Millard Erickson, *Christian Theology*, (Grand Rapids: Baker, 1998), 1099-1100.

[13] Ibid, 1100.

themselves to saving faith in Jesus. No one is baptized in the New Testament examples who did not first confess Christ. Second, the New Testament demands that salvation through Jesus occurs before baptism. Scripture texts such as Matthew 28:19 and Acts 2:37-41 provide the framework: salvation first and then baptism.[14]

Furthermore, the generally accepted mode of baptism is immersion in water. This is evident in the meaning of the word *baptize*: "As recognized by all Greek lexicons, *baptizo* means to dip, submerge or immerse."[15] The Greek prepositions used with the word *baptizo* also indicate immersion as the biblical mode of baptism: "Jesus was baptized by John *in* (eis) the Jordan (Mark 1:9)."[16] And baptism by immersion also best symbolizes Spirit baptism where the one who was spiritually dead is brought to life in Christ (Rom. 6:4).

Communion

Just as the Lord commanded His disciples to go and "gospel-ize" the world, baptizing those who believe, He also commanded them to observe communion, also known as the Lord's Table or Supper. The Lord instituted this ordinance as part of the last supper He experienced with His disciples before His death. Luke records that the early church observed this ordinance by breaking bread together (Acts 2:42).

Later, the apostle Paul reminds the Corinthian church of the importance of proper communion, stating that it was very important for them to avoid anything connected with idols. Referring to the bread and drink which are part of the communion ordinance (1 Cor. 10:16), he warns that a combination of fellowship with pagans in their religious feasts and then communion with Christians at the Lord's Table was impossible to justify: "How can you drink the cup of demons and the cup of the Lord?" (1 Cor. 10:21).

---

[14] Ibid, 1106.
[15] Rolland McCune, *A Systematic Theology of Biblical Christianity*, (Detroit: Detroit Baptist Theological Seminary, 2010), 3: 271.
[16] Ibid.

The importance of communion is twofold. First, it memorializes the death of Jesus. The Lord's body was broken on the cross at Calvary. His blood was shed for the remission of sins. By partaking in communion, the church *remembers* this incredible sacrifice of Jesus on behalf of His people. Second, the elements of communion symbolize this sacrifice: the bread represents His body, and the juice represents His blood. Belief in Jesus, the Lord told us, is essentially what it means to eat His body and drink His blood (Jn. 6:35, 53-57).[17]

Some argue that only church members should observe communion. This is called "closed communion." Closed communion does not allow all believers to take the elements, but only those who are members of that local church and in good standing.[18] Another view is "open communion" that sees this ordinance as part of individual worship, similar to giving. The church does not exercise authority over what people give to the Lord; likewise, in open communion the church merely presents the elements and leaves it up to individuals to partake or not. Such churches explain that salvation is the only requirement for participation in the communion ordinance. Other churches practice communion that lies somewhere between open and closed.[19]

Whether a church practices closed, open, or some modified position on communion, the primary emphasis is that those who take communion are worshipping God as believers in Christ and as part of their fellowship with other believers in a local church.

Communion also encourages unity in among church members. Disunity was one of the significant problems in the Corinthian church. It was so bad, that Paul states their gathering together, something they were to be doing regularly as a church (see chapter 2), was actually making things worse (1 Cor. 11:17). The factions in the Church of Corinth

---

[17] See Rolland McCune, *A Systematic Theology of Biblical Christianity*, 3: 279-80. McCune identifies the importance of prophecy, noting that communion is to be observed until He comes back. He also provides helpful discussion of some of the false positions on communion taken by Roman Catholics and other denominations.

[18] Ibid, 285.

[19] Our church follows a moderating position between open and closed communion. We allow non-members to take communion, but strongly admonish them that this is based on their being members of a church of like faith and practice. We do not limit the distribution of the elements to members only, but we also do not give them out to every non-member without some instructions on whether they should partake of communion with us or not.

(1:11-12) were apparently most evident during their communion service. Instead of demonstrating Christ's love for each other, something that is central to the gospel message and obvious in the sacrifice of Jesus, they were showing their mutual disdain for one another. They were eating and drinking the communion elements "unworthily," something Paul warns was endangering themselves (11:29-30). He encourages them to self-examination in order to see if they were actually coming to the communion service with the right spirit (v. 28).

Christ Exalted

All of these elements of worship (prayer, music, reading Scripture, giving offerings, preaching, and observing the ordinances) are intended to one goal—the exaltation of Jesus Christ. As the early church hymn indicates, God the Father has given Jesus a name above all other names. At His name every knee should bow and every tongue should confess that He is both Lord and Christ. There should never be a time when believers just "go through the motions" of worship without deeply contemplating the meaning of their songs and prayers, the point of the sermon, the opportunity to give back to God. Christians worship the God of all the universe, the God of creation. What is truly amazing is that He even recognizes our worship. To Him be glory in the church … (Eph. 3:21).

Discipleship Questions

1. Which of the elements of worship mean the most to you personally? Why?

2. Should a church "innovate" by adding new elements to foster a more "worshipful" experience?

3. Should Christians perform the ordinances outside of a church service? For example, is it okay for a Christian to baptize a new convert in a public pool (not a church service)?

4. Why might it be problematic for non-church members to take communion?

Chapter 5

Church Membership

O N April 18, 2019, Gallup released data from a poll regarding the number of Americans who "belong" to a church. The results reveal that church membership is declining in the United States. In the late 1990s, 73% of people who self-describe as religious were part of a church (any religion or denomination). Twenty years later, that number is down to 64%.[1] Even worse, the number of young adults belonging to a church is a fraction of what it once was. Every church growth scholar expects American church membership to continue to decline.

One reason for the decrease in church membership is that many Christians no longer believe membership is important. They often point to the concept of the "universal church," claiming that it is enough to be part of the family of God. But being part of God's family does not eliminate the biblical mandate that Christians belong organically to a local church body.

The Concept of Church Membership

It is popular to refer to the church as a "voluntary organization." It *is* voluntary in the sense that the American government does not mandate

---

[1] Bob Smietana and Aysha Khan, "Gallup: Number of Americans who belong to a church or house of worship plummets," accessed May 1, 2019, https://religionnews.com/2019/04/18/gallup-number-of-americans-who-belong-to-a-church-or-house-of-worship-plummets/.

church membership. Participation is a personal choice: We live in a free, democratic society where our religious liberty allows individuals to choose if or when to join a church. However, membership in a true, biblical, Christian church is not simply a matter of volunteering like a suburban mom volunteers in the PTA of her local elementary school.

New Testament Assumption

There is a strong assumption in the New Testament that all believers submit themselves to others within a local church. How else can Paul's command for mutual submission be carried out (Eph. 5:21)? If there is no church membership, then Christians are free to pick and choose to whom they will submit. This takes the teeth out of Paul's command.

For those who claim that church membership is not mandated, it should be noted that the *assumption* of church membership is presented in Scripture in the same manner as other assumptions, such as the existence of God and the doctrine of the Trinity. No professed Christian denies God's existence and few question the Trinity. Neither should we deny the importance of joining a local church. The assumption of church membership is demonstrated biblically in at least seven ways.

- First, when Luke states that three thousand were saved at Pentecost (Acts 2), and that later, five thousand were saved (Acts 4), these are not fabricated figures. Luke is describing documented information about the early church.

- Second, Paul's admonition to Timothy about the importance of the Ephesian believers only supporting "true" widows referred to a registry of widows in that church (1 Tim. 5:9).

- Third, the institution of deacons involved the people in Jerusalem choosing out from among their own group those who would lead in caring for the needy (Acts 6).

· Fourth, the church in Antioch was gathered in prayer when God selected Paul and Barnabas for their missionary journey. They selected the two men out of their membership.

· Fifth, Paul's command to the Corinthians to expel the immoral and unrepentant man from the congregation implied some sort of membership.

· Sixth, the fact that Paul refers to the local church as a body implies that there are church members. The members (of the body) are *members* (of the church).[2]

· Seventh, the word pastor (*poimen*) means shepherd. The pastor is the shepherd of the flock. The reference to a church as a flock of sheep with a shepherd implies membership. Good shepherds knew their sheep. They did not shepherd sheep they did not personally know.

While there is no "thou shalt be a member of a local church" command in the New Testament, the evidence is very strong that it is God's intended will for every believer to be connected by membership to a local church.[3]

The Basis of Membership

Most biblical churches have always maintained as one of their distinctives that membership in a local church is based on a profession of salvation by faith in Jesus and subsequent water (believer's) baptism.[4]

---

[2] The entire idea of a person who is part of a church is a member comes from this. The word member means "limb." For a better explanation, see https://www.etymonline.com/word/member.

[3] Rolland McCune, *A Systematic Theology of Biblical Christianity*, 3: 226-227.

[4] The earliest Baptists emphasized some of the core Christian doctrines such as the Trinity, the inspiration and authority of Scripture, the blood atonement of Jesus, and the doctrine of the church including the necessity of water baptism. See H. Leon McBeth, *The Baptist Heritage: Four Centuries of Baptist Witness*, 69-91. The Baptist Distinctives, a formulation of Baptist

"One important point that Baptists derive from the Scriptures regarding the local church is the makeup of its constituency."[5]

Salvation

The New Testament explains that the relationship between believers is based on mutual salvation in Christ. John proclaimed the "word of life" in order to have a partnership (*koinonia*) with those who believed his message (1 Jn. 1:1-3). "There is an element of participation in some spiritual gift or in Christian service, and there is the element of union with other believers as a result of common enjoyment of some spiritual privilege."[6] In fact, John states that the same fellowship he had with God the Father and Jesus Christ he also had with fellow believers (v. 3).

There are many who profess to be "Christians," but some are false. John's tests of spiritual life in 1 John indicate five important proofs of salvation.

· Confessing one's sins (1:9) rather than confessing to have no sin or to never have sinned (1:8, 10)

· Keeping the commands of Jesus (2:3-4)

· Ordering one's character and conduct to be like the Lord's (2:6)

· Loving other brothers and sisters in Christ (2:9-10)

· Acknowledging the truth about Jesus as the Christ (2:22-23)

---

orthopraxy often follows the acronym BAPTIST including (1) Biblical authority, (2) Autonomy of the local church, (3) Priesthood of the believer, (4) Two ordinances, (5) Individual soul liberty, (6) Saved, baptized membership, (7) Two offices—pastor(s) and deacon(s), and (8) Separation of Church and State. See

https://www.garbc.org/about-us/beliefs-constitution/baptist-distinctives/.

[5] This statement is attributed to Richard Weeks, accessed May 1, 2019, https://www.mbu.edu/seminary/the-logic-of-brapsis/.

[6] I. Howard Marshall, "The Epistles of John," *New International Commentary on the New Testament*, 104.

So, membership in a local church group is only possible for those who have joined together in this unity of repentance and faith in Christ according to His Word. If we gather regularly with others who have accepted His salvation, it is logical that we should become members of a group together.

Water-Baptism

The word Baptist comes from the words "baptism" and "baptize." Two of the seven Baptist distinctives involve baptism, more than any other doctrine. Baptists are big on baptism! Baptism signifies the indwelling Holy Spirit, proclaims the baptized saint as having accepted the gospel for salvation, and demonstrates submission to follow Christ.[7]

The acclaimed first missionary from the Americas, Adoniram Judson, began a translation of the New Testament from Greek while in route from New England to India. He had been ordained and commissioned by Congregationalists in New England. These were godly people, but they were not Baptists. When Judson translated the word "baptism" (*baptizo*), he came to a life-changing point of decision. "Adoniram had been baptized as an infant in the Congregational way, by the sprinkling of a few drops of water on his head."[8] He became convinced that the Congregationalists were wrong about baptism. His wife, a lifelong Congregationalist, was not very pleased by his "discovery." Even worse, his commissioning board was Congregationalist and expected him to perform baptisms according to their accepted beliefs. Regardless, knowing that they might lose both financial and prayer support, the Judsons were baptized (thus becoming Baptists) by William Ward in Calcutta on September 6, 1812.[9]

---

[7] Larry Oats, unpublished notes "Ecclesiology," Maranatha Baptist Seminary. Dr. Oats also comments on infant baptism as being unscriptural and notes that many Baptists have replaced infant baptism with infant dedication, a practice that is not found in the Bible. He writes: "The risk of infant dedication is that it is a created activity which seems to indicate that adult baptism is insufficient for the church."

[8] Courtney Anderson, *To the Golden Shore*, 127.

[9] Evan D. Burns, "The Best Sermon upon Baptism that I have ever Heard," accessed May 1, 2019, http://andrewfullercenter.org/blog/blog/2013/10/the-best-sermon-upon-baptism-that-i-have-ever-heard.

Adoniram Judson recognized what we also see as significant for members of a local church: that believer's baptism demonstrates an individual's relationship to Christ and is therefore significant for the believer's membership in that local group of believers.

The Nine Commitments of Membership

Once a Christian makes profession of salvation by faith in Jesus and is baptized by immersion (or by other means if immersion is impossible),[10] that person can become an official part of—member of—a local church. In doing so, he takes upon himself nine important commitments as a member of a local body of Christ.

Commitment 1: Maintain Doctrinal Purity. Church members are called to protect the church against false doctrine. By studying God's Word together, members affirm what Scripture teaches and deny what it condemns. Many churches have been undone because of church members who are weak on Bible doctrine. It is true that there are pastors, like wolves, whose doctrine harms the God's flock (Acts 20:29). However, these are only tolerated in congregations where Bible doctrine is not emphasized.

Commitment 2: Follow Pastoral Leadership.[11] Church members should not be "lemmings," following their leader off the proverbial cliff. However, as the pastor is true to Scripture, members should be true and loyal in following his leadership. Pastors are not dictators, but undershepherds who serve as the servants of Jesus to the church. Pastors are called to care for God's sheep willingly, regardless of their compensation (1 Pet. 5:2) and live as examples for others (1 Pet. 5: 3; 1 Cor. 11:1). Church members should follow them willingly. Too many pastors have suffered terribly at the hands of their fellow congregants.

Commitment 3: Partner Interdependently. Church members should work together to advance the cause of Jesus, thinking of their relationship with one another as a partnership. This is evident in the way

---

[10] There are times when total immersion may be impossible. For example, physical infirmity may prevent total immersion in water. At these times, the principle of baptism is best expressed through water baptism by other means.

[11] The remaining commitments provide an outline to the rest of this book.

Paul describes Philemon as his "coworker" (Ph. 1:1). He calls Apphia "beloved," and both he and Archippus are "brothers in arms" (v. 2). He refers to Onesimus, Philemon's runaway servant, as indispensable to his ministry (v. 11). Epaphras is his prison companion (v. 23). Mark, Aristarchus, Demas, and Luke are "co-laborers" (v. 24). Even more profound is how Paul describes his ministry team to the church in Colossae (Col. 4:9-14). Paul was not a maverick or a one-man-band: He worked closely with other believers for Christ.

Commitment 4: Help Each Other Spiritually. The ministry of providing spiritual help (*paraclesis*) to other believers is similar to the ministry of the Holy Spirit (*paraclete*). This is how the Thessalonian church interacted with one another. Paul exhorted them to encourage each other regarding their spiritual walk with Christ (1 Thess. 4:1). At the same time, they were to provide hope for those who were in grief over the death of loved ones (v. 18). Both actions, though really quite different emotionally, are part of the same process. Everyone needs someone to come alongside and give encouragement when they are struggling spiritually. We also have times when we need comfort because of sorrow over loss. Both are equally important. This is what church members are to do for each other.

Commitment 5: Utilize Talents and Gifts. It is very easy for Christians to become lazy or selfish when it comes to life in the church. No one wants to do the "dirty" jobs or be responsible for difficult people. But God has given each believer certain abilities that others do not have (1 Cor. 12:4-30). Some can sing. Others can organize and manage. Others are great with people. And others are able to do more mundane tasks, like pulling weeds in the parking lot. God has also gifted each believer with spiritual gifts that are outside his normal capability. These gifts enable that person to do specific spiritual work within the church. Church members can and should invest themselves in Christian service by being actively involved in God's work according to the capabilities God has given them.

Commitment 6: Be Accountable to Each Other. Holding others accountable is not very fun. Few people enjoy confrontation. However, the New Testament explains that the local church should be more involved in decisions when people stray from faithfulness to Christ (1 Cor. 5-6). Sometimes this accountability for each other could even mean expelling a member from the congregation, acknowledging that his profession of faith in Christ is not genuine when compared to his refusal to repent over his immoral behavior.

Commitment 7: Support the Church Financially. The church is not a credit union and should not be involved in business like companies designed to make a profit. However, it requires financial support to keep a church operational and in good standing in the community. Church members should make regular contributions, funding local church planting and global evangelism efforts, helping those who are needy in the church, and supporting the financial needs of building or maintaining church facilities.

Commitment 8: Engage the Community for Christ. Every church is an embassy of the kingdom of heaven to a foreign kingdom (unsaved humanity). It is the local church's responsibility to reach out to its community in order to develop redemptive relationships. These relationships provide a platform to give the gospel of Jesus and help believers to share a testimony of how Christ's followers live. This kind of engagement is crucial for the church to be relevant as it seeks to further the gospel locally.

Commitment 9: Advance the Mission of Christ Globally. God is passionate about missions. The second commission of Jesus to His disciples was a command to expand the reach of their previous mission from the villages around Galilee and in Judea (Luke 9-10) to the ends of the earth (Matt. 28:19-20). Furthermore, they were to go to everyone, not just to the Jews. The gospel of Jesus must be proclaimed to every person regardless of race or ethnicity, regardless of economic status or social level. New local churches must be established around the world.

Opposition to Membership

The nine commitments of church members are important. Unfortunately, not every church member is in agreement with all nine. They choose which of these they will follow and ignore the rest as if the church is a banquet table. Specifically, there are three obstacles to healthy church membership.

Unrepentant sin. When church members live in sin, particularly gross sin, and refuse to repent over that sin, the effect strains the entire body of Christ. Like cancer that eats at one place on the human body but threatens survival of the whole, so unrepentant sin threatens the whole church. Paul refers to this sin as "leaven" (1 Cor. 5:6-7). The housewife baking bread needs to add only a little yeast to her dough, and the whole lump will eventually be leavened. The influence of gross sin on a church is profound.

Divisions and Cliques. Every individual relates better to some church members than others. Some church members relate like human sandpaper, and any close contact painfully rubs off a layer of skin. Proverbs provides counsel for dealing with difficult people: encourage them to love (10:12), be patient (12:16), recognize the problems that come with quarrelling (17:14), avoid situations that cause strife (20:3), and do not become friends with hot-tempered people (22:24). But divisions can develop in the church as people form cliques with those they like, avoiding those they do not like. This is not a healthy interdependence. And we should never cultivate a love for the wealthy at the expense of the poor (Jam. 2:1-4).

Unresolved Interpersonal Conflict. It is likely that the reason many leave a church for another in the same town is that they have conflicts with others that have gone unresolved for a long time. These conflicts are like open wounds that fester. They do not heal, but instead provide a source of pain (or at least discomfort) when the two in conflict come into contact. Church members are to be "of the same mind in the Lord" (Phil. 4:2). The command of Jesus is that conflict between members must be resolved. The offended party must confront the offender without becoming a gossip (Matt. 18:15). If the conflict cannot be resolved between the two, church leadership must get involved to help them reconcile (vv. 16-17).[12]

---

[12] My personal experience as a pastor suggests that most people leave a church because of

Sign Me Up

The United States military is a volunteer service. Therefore, the military branches advertise in order to recruit new servicemembers. The most famous recruitment poster displays Uncle Sam, telling young men that he wants them to enlist in the Army during World War I. The white-haired, bearded man is seen pointing his finger with the caption "I Want You" overhead. The message of the poster is direct: Young men were needed for the war effort.[13]

The Church is also at war. At this present time, Satan and his army control the world (1 Jn. 5:19). He is the "prince of the power of the air" who is now "working in the children of disobedience" (Eph. 2:2). God has called His people to join up for the spiritual fight (Eph. 6:10-20). We are the Church militant. God is calling everyone who professes salvation in Christ to be part of His local army, the local church. His recruiting call to eternal life in the future comes with a life of spiritual military service here in the present.

Discipleship Questions

1. Are you a member of a church? If not, why not?

2. Are you keeping the nine commitments of church membership? If you are not, please explain why that is.

3. Which of the nine commitments is most difficult to maintain?

4. How might your church membership be compared to an enlistment in God's army?

---

unresolved conflict. Of course, this refers to those who leave a church and find another church in the same town. Teaching believers how to resolve conflicts with others is a good way of maintaining a healthy membership.

[13] See https://amhistory.si.edu/militaryhistory/collection/object.asp?ID=548, accessed May 17, 2019.

Chapter 6

Pastoral Leadership

I N both Ephesians and Colossians, the apostle Paul uses a term to describe the importance of Jesus to the church. Paul refers to Jesus as the "head." This is clearly what Paul means when he states that Jesus is "the head over all things to the church, which is His body..." (Eph. 1:22-23). He repeats this truth later in Ephesians referring to Jesus as "the head of the church" (Eph. 5:2). Likewise, he tells the Colossians saints that Jesus is "head of the body, the church..." (Col. 1:18). There is a vital relationship between head and body. A person can lose some body parts and remain alive. This is presently impossible when it comes to the head. This is why Paul states that the unbelieving philosophers in Colossae were guilty of "not holding the head" which is a problem because from the head "all the body by joints and bands having nourishments ministered and knit together, increases with the increase of God" (Col. 2:19). In other words, the head is primary. Everything begins with the head. Church leadership begins with Jesus Christ. He is the leader in every true church. This is not just a statement of formality. Jesus is the true vine. We are only branches (Jn. 15:5).

The consequence of this truth is that Jesus alone has preeminence. Paul bases this truth on two important reasons. (1) Jesus is supreme because He is the creator (Col. 1:16-18). He writes that Jesus created all things in heaven and earth whether they are visible or not. He states plainly that "all things were created by Him and for Him" (v. 17). Moreover, all of the created world rely on Him for its subsistence. Thus, Jesus is "the head of the body, the church...." (2) Not only is

Jesus supreme because He is the creator, but He is supreme because he also gave up Himself in order to save the church (Eph. 5:25). This reference to redemption is important because it explains that Jesus has more than just creative authority and prerogative. He has moral authority over the church because He purchased it with His own blood. This is like the little boy who bought the toy boat he made in a pawn shop.[1] Jesus has authority both as creator and owner.[2]

Undershepherds

Because Jesus leads the church, He has the right to set up positions of authority in His church to be a visible representation of His leadership. This individual(s)[3] is a gift to from the Lord Jesus to the church (Eph. 4:11). The pastor is a shepherd of God's flock and is responsible to provide spiritual food to meet the needs of God's sheep, the church (Acts 20:28). Even as Jesus is the Good Shepherd who gave up His life for the church (John 10:11), so the pastor is an undershepherd. He serves by the will of Jesus, the Chief Shepherd (1 Pet. 5:4).

In the New Testament, the pastor is specifically identified by three titles and possibly a fourth. The three titles are overseer (episcopos), elder (presbuteros), and pastor/shepherd (poimain). They all refer to the same man—a pastor is a shepherd, elder, and overseer. The fourth possible title is angel (*angellos*) which means messenger (Rev. 1-3).[4] From these titles, the duties and requirements of the office of a pastor emerge. A pastor oversees the church, he is a leader within it, and functions as the one who provides spiritual guidance. Moreover, he has a message to give to the congregation from the Lord. He is the "preacher."

---

[1] The way the story goes is that a little boy builds a toy boat and loses it on a lake. Some days later, he sees the same boat for sale in a pawn shop. He saves up his money to buy back his own boat. Grasping the little boat in his hands, he says to it: "you're my boat. I made you and I bought you."

[2] Earl Radmacher notes some of the important truths that arise from the head to body relationship between Jesus and the church. He notes unity with the head, sustenance, and interdependence of the body itself. See Radmacher, *The Nature of the Church*, pp. 237-238.

[3] The potentiality represented by the plural (s) is because a church may have more than one pastor. From this point forward, that assumption will be made even though the singular is used.

[4] The angels of the 7 churches in Revelation were most likely the pastors.

Qualifications

One of the most difficult aspects of qualifications is whether or not it is God's will for someone to pastor.[5] Many men have sought the office of a pastor or remained in the pastorate even while being sinfully disqualified by virtue of claiming to be called. Others have rejected God's leading because of this same subjective calling. The fact is, the New Testament does not use the term *call* in relation to becoming a pastor. "Nowhere does the word call appear in the biblical record in connection with pastoral ministry."[6] An examination of the New Testament term (kaleo—verb meaning "I call") reveals that the word is used in various ways, but *never* in calling someone to pastoral ministry. "What is strikingly absent, however, is any demonstrable NT use of the term in the sense of a *mystical call to ministry* sometimes anticipating in ordination council meetings."[7]

So, how can we know if God is *leading* a man to be a pastor? The first step in answering that question is entirely subjective. Does the candidate have an innate desire to pastoral leadership? The apostle Paul indicates that a pastor should internally covet the biblical office itself (1 Tim. 3:1). That is, after learning what it is that pastors do, the individual should want to be one. Some who train pastors in Bible college or seminary say something like this: "if you can do anything else other than be a pastor, then you should." What they are saying is that if a person is not fully committed to being a pastor, he will eventually desert his office because of difficulty, trial, or even persecution.[8]

---

[5] Some of the confusion is the result of theologians conflating the office of prophet (OT) with the office of pastor (NT). While some principles may be derived from Old Testament texts pertaining to the pastorate (or deaconate), there is not really any one-for-one correlation between Old Testament leaders and leaders in the New Testament church.

[6] Mark Snoeberger, unpublished notes on Ecclesiology, Detroit Baptist Theological Seminary, p. 46.

[7] Ibid.

[8] Personally, I have found the reverse to be true. There are many other things I could do and hopefully would be good at doing. But, there is nothing else that I want to do. Pastoring is what I love. It is my life. I would rather not live if I could not pastor. That's the "desire" that Paul refers to in 1 Tim. 3:1. I cannot explain where that desire came from originally other than to say that it must be that God put it into my heart. Such an internal motivation is what keeps pastors serving even during difficult times.

After answering the question of personal desire, both 1 Timothy and Titus provide information on whether or not the candidate is qualified to pursue vocational ministry. A study of these texts reveal that pastoral qualifications settle on three separate areas: character, conduct, and giftedness. Two of these areas is controlled by the individual himself (character and conduct) and the other is given to Him by God (spiritual gifts).

Character. There are two words that express the necessary character of a man who aspires to be a pastor. Both words are translated "blameless." He must be unreproachable (*anepilemptos*) (1 Tim. 3:2). "Just like Daniel in OT times (see Dan. 6:4), this person must be a man of integrity against whom no legitimate charge can be brought."[9] The word itself conveys the idea that there is nothing in the individual's life that can be held onto. Like the smooth face of a towering rock, the pastor's character should have nothing to which any charge can take hold. This does not mean that the pastor is sinless. Only the Lord Jesus was without sin. Rather, it means that the pastor's character is one where he cannot be rebuked. The second word (*anegkletos*) means that no accuser can come forward with a charge against him (Tit. 1:6). There cannot be anything in the pastor's life that someone can use as a charge of moral sin against him. That the pastor is above reproach is non-negotiable. In both passages, Paul uses the word "must" to highlight how important character is regarding pastoral qualifications. This is not something that can be overlooked. A pastor's skill in preaching, his organizational ability, his charismatic personality, or his ability to build a growing ministry do not compensate for failure in moral character. It is likely that one of the reasons that Paul includes such a strong emphasis on the pastor's personal character is that the false teachers were notoriously lacking in moral character.[10]

Conduct. Out of a life of strong moral character there arises a pastoral demeanor, conduct that befits the high office of God's ambassador, of

---

[9] Kostenberger, Andres. *Biblical Commentary for Christian Proclamation,* "1-2 Timothy & Titus." p. 126.

[10] See 2 Peter 2 and Jude for a description of the moral sin of the false teachers who plagued the early church.

the undershepherd to the Chief Shepherd Jesus Christ. He is God's steward managing the affairs of His church (*oikonomos*) (Tit. 1:7).

Faithful. A pastor must be husband (*aner*) to one wife (*gyne*). There is a lot of debate about what this means. There is no possible way to translate *aner* and *gyne* any differently than husband and wife. Thus, unless one unravels the basic meaning of language, a pastor must be a man. As to his marital status, there are four possible answers. (1) *Husband* (note: the word is not "man" but "husband") may require that the pastor be married. This position precludes a single man being elevated to the position of pastor. (2) The word "one" (*mia*) might mean that the pastor can only marry once in his lifetime. Thus, when a pastor's wife dies, he is not free to remarry and remain a pastor.[11] (3) This position prohibits someone being a pastor if he has been divorced. (4) This position holds that the pastor must be presently faithful to the spouse that he has. This is the most likely interpretation of what Paul means.

Sensible. An important quality for the pastor is stability. Some pastors are always moving and changing. They are always trying to find the next big thing. This is not what God has in mind for the leader of His church. The pastor should be temperate in his spirit meaning he is not rash in his decisions.[12] He should be sensible in judgment. He should be self-controlled, curbing his passions in order to behave rightly. His conduct should be considered modest and orderly. At the same time, he should abstain from any intoxication, even if ever so slight.

Friendly. Friendliness is required for someone who is going to lead a church in discipleship. A pastor cannot just hole up in his study, refusing to make friends with the members in his church. In fact, his friendliness should be one of the obvious features that mark his conduct. People should know that he is a friendly guy. He should have a willingness to talk to strangers.[13] At the same time, he must not be easily angry or arrogant. His ministry is to teach the truth to others. At times, teaching the truth leads to conflict. Disagreements can make

---

[11] If both positions 1 and 2 are held simultaneously, then the pastor whose wife dies must leave the pastorate.

[12] This term actually means to abstain from wine, something reiterated in 1 Tim. 3:3. Alcohol as a recreational beverage has no place in the pastor's lifestyle.

[13] Funny thing, his wife should probably complain that he speaks to strangers too much!

people disagreeable. In such situations, the pastor should be mild-mannered. He should not quarrel with others, getting into fights. He should not be "hot-tempered." Pastors should not be naturally violent men. Rather, he should be mild and gentle with others, not hot-tempered.

Finances. He should not be a greedy person who seeks to be wealthy. He should not be known as someone who loves money and the lifestyle it affords. Jesus taught that one cannot serve God and money at the same time (Matt. 6:24). It is unseemly for the pastor to be laying up treasure on earth when he should be teaching the opposite to his congregation.[14] He should demonstrate stability and self-control when it comes to budgeting, saving, and spending.

Family. There are so many examples of pastors who have failed in the area of family that the children of pastors have their own acronym PK (MK for the children of missionaries). It is true that men who invest their energy into building the church can neglect their families to their own detriment. The pastor should oversee his private affairs in a way that brings honor to God. If he has children living in his home, they should be living in obedience to him. Titus refers to the children as "faithful" (*pistos*) indicating that older children living at home should have a Christian testimony of salvation. Furthermore, these children should not be living a morally wicked lifestyle rejecting the leadership of their father.

Maturity. It would also be a mistake to elevate someone to the office of pastor if he is a new Christian. A recent convert is not ready to be a pastor. It takes time for someone to mature in his Christian life. It takes time to develop habits that are right and that observe the commands of Scripture. Piety is a life-long pursuit and no neophyte to the Christian life can be expected to be a leader in this area.[15] It is impossible. Furthermore, maturity in character and conduct must be accompanied by maturity in handling God's Word. Those who do not

---

[14] This does not mean that a pastor cannot have money (savings) or nice things (from being disciplined with his money). Sometimes the greediest are also the poorest.

[15] My pastor (when I was a child) used to say after the congregation sang the hymn *Take Time to be Holy* that "it takes time to be holy." Holiness comes from a long time with God. It is not something that happens overnight.

know the Bible very well can do great damage in the church. People training to be pastors should be given opportunities to practice, but this should be in a controlled environment with pastoral oversight.

Testimony. Finally, the pastor should have a good testimony with unbelievers in the community. If unbelievers do not respect the pastor as a man of character and good conduct, he cannot lead the church in that community.[16]

Giftedness. While a man may have some control over his own character and conduct, only God gifts a person for pastoral work. This is not something a seminary education can replace. One cannot simply educate himself to the point of spiritual giftedness. The pastor is God's gift to the church (Eph. 4:11). God endows him with spiritual gifts suited for the responsibility of pastoring. For example, it is likely that a pastor will be gifted with the ability to administrate (1 Cor. 12:28) and to lead (Rom. 12:8).[17] It is also necessary for the pastor to have the gift of teaching (see 1 Cor. 12 and Rom. 12). Teaching does not mean that the pastor is necessarily a charismatic speaker. It means that God uses his teaching, even if he is a little boring, to bring spiritual change in the lives of his congregation.

Ordination

The traditionally formal entrance into a life of vocational ministry is ordination. This has been used in the past as a kind of entrance exam that once it is finished, the man who is ordained is deemed forever qualified to serve in pastoral office. This is not what God intends. Ordination in Scripture is to a particular office in a particular church (Tit. 1:5). Once an ordained pastor leaves his ministry, he relinquishes his pastoral authority conferred on him by ordination. If he chooses to reenter pastoral ministry afterward, even if this is almost immediately afterward (think of a pastor transitioning from one church to another), he should be reexamined as to his fitness for pastoral service. Most

---

[16] Sometimes pastors make mistakes that might preclude them from leading in their present church, whereas he might be able to lead a different church in a different community.

[17] See Wayne Grudem, *Systematic Theology.* p. 1020.

churches do this by way of examination of a new pastor candidate and give authority to the new pastor in the formal installation service. The idea, however, that "once-ordained-always-ordained" is not biblical.

It is also problematic that most ordination councils focus on the doctrinal statement of the man seeking pastoral ordination and virtually ignore questions about character, conduct, and giftedness.[18] While doctrine is important, these other qualities are just as important. The standard to be a pastor is an extraordinarily a high bar.

Fakes

There are two types of fake or false pastors and churches do well to avoid them. The first fake is the "false" pastor. While he might appear to be true, he is really a wolf wearing the clothing of sheep (Matt. 7:15). Paul uses this term "wolf" warning the Ephesian pastors that false teachers would arise in their congregation (Acts 20:29).

The second kind of fake pastor is the one who "pretends" to be a spiritual leader. He is willing to lead while things are going well, when church life is tranquil. But when problems arise, such men flee the scene leaving church members the responsibility of sorting out the mess by themselves. The Bible calls such pseudo-pastors "hirelings" (*misthotos*). They are not a shepherds, but rather hired to do shepherd work. Jesus describes these as cowardly in the face of opposition (Jn. 10:12). Hirelings serve as long as they can make money. Their emphasis is on income, not on feeding and protecting God's flock.

The Relationship Between Pastor(s) and Church Members

One of the most important relationships within the church is between pastor and church member. There is a sense in which the pastor is a part of the church family. He attends the church with his wife and family. Their names are in the directory. At the same time, there is something

---

[18] For more information about the process of ordination, see Appendix 3.

separate about the pastor from the rest of the people. He thinks about them differently from the way they think about him. Their burdens keep him up at night; they turn him to prayer. He knows that he must give an account of them to God (Heb. 13:17).

Shoulder-to-shoulder

The best pastor-church member relationship is one in which both work together to advance God's work. A good pastor is not "above" the church like a leader of industry watching over his business and the lowly workers in the shop. He works alongside them day by day to help them grow in their Christian walk. They do the same for him. While the office of pastor is formal and there are accompanying responsibilities that are different from the typical layman, the relationship between pastor and church member is should be friendly. There should be a sense that pastors and church members are co-laborers for Christ.

Congregational rule

Church members must also keep in mind that the pastor is not the church's king. The pastor's wife is not its queen. There are no "first ladies" in the church. That is just something man came up with to elevate the pastor above the position found in Scripture.[19] In a healthy church, there is strong pastoral *leadership* that works in tandem with congregational *rule*. This is demonstrated in the way Paul addresses churches, and can be seen in John's epistles, particularly 2 John. The New Testament approach to church leadership is pastors lead within the confines of congregational rule.

Voluntary submission

The way in which a church member submits himself to pastoral leadership is in his willingness to be taught by the pastor. It would be kind of a strange sight to envision a flock of sheep eating the grass on the field

---

[19] A church with this mindset is open to pastoral abuse, something that is more common than it should be in our evangelical culture.

of an unknown shepherd. With all of the technological advances of our civilization, it is possible to follow the ministries of other men. Sometimes, these men are not pastors or worse, they do not even qualify to be a pastor. Yet they disseminate their teaching on the radio, television, or on the internet. The Bible does not envision this as a healthy activity for church members as a rule. God commands church members to "be persuaded" by their own pastor(s), not by someone they really do not know who has a large media ministry (Heb. 13:17).

Mutual submission

The best churches are those where both pastor(s) and church members submit themselves to Christ as the leader of the assembly (1 Pet. 5:1-5). In doing so, both fulfill necessary roles and functions that make the body of Christ into what God desires, and bring glory to Him (Eph. 3:21). When this occurs, the church operates in such a way that each of its body parts is doing exactly what God intends. The pastor is faithfully shepherding God's flock and the church members are feeding on what God provides them through His gifts to them.

Discipleship Questions

1. Why is it important that Christians consider Jesus as the head of the church?

2. Why is it important that we get away from the sense of a mystical call? How might this idea be abused?

3. If a man is not perfectly qualified (let's say his finances are out of whack), can he still be a pastor? Explain your answer.

4. Do you think the gift of preaching/teaching means a pastor will be an exciting speaker?

Chapter 7

The Ministry of Deacons

O NE of the most vital, yet misunderstood roles in the church, is the ministry of deacons. Churches wrestle with questions such as: what are the deacon's responsibilities? Do deacons "hire" the pastor? Do deacons serve lifetime appointments? Is there such a thing as a "deacon board?" Can anyone be a deacon, or is it an office reserved to men? Should deacons be ordained?

The Establishment of Deacon Ministry

While there is not universal agreement, it is generally assumed that the first deacons were appointed during the conflict of the widows in Acts 6. The church in Jerusalem was very ethnically diverse, a result of an early dispersion of the Jews into the Greco-Roman world.[1] This ethnic diversity caused some tension between the Hebraic Jews who mainly spoke Aramaic and the Hellenist Jews who mainly spoke Greek.[2] As has often proven true throughout Church History, major interpersonal relationship problems that were under the surface in the Jerusalem church bubbled up because of a seemingly insignificant problem. Apparently the Greek speaking believers charged the Aramaic speaking Christians with ignoring their widows. This was not a

---

[1] Stewart Custer, *Witness to Christ: A Commentary on Acts*, (Greenville, SC: Bob Jones University Press, 2000), p. 76.

[2] F. F. Bruce, "The Book of Acts," *The New International Commentary on the New Testament*, (Grand Rapids: Eerdmans, 1975), p. 128.

purposeful neglect but one that came as a result of the language barrier.[3] Luke writes that this neglect caused the Hellenist Christians to murmur (*goggysmos*) against the others. This kind of division threatened to split the church, a serious threat to unity in the first church established after Jesus ascended into heaven.

When the apostles (the twelve) learned of the problem, they called the church together (church members were called disciples) to offer a solution to the problem. It can be safely assumed that their solution was discussed at length between them before this public announcement, though Luke does not mention their private deliberations.[4] Their solution was a new office in the church, the office of deacon. This solution is unique to the church. The synagogue had elders, something the church borrowed into its own polity, but deacons are something totally new.[5] The deacon's role was to administrate the distribution of church funds to the widows in fairness to each (Acts 6:3).

The Deacon's Duties

The most common way biblical churches presently understand deacon ministry is that they are the church's governing board. "Many Bible-believing churches … have made the diaconate the ruling board of the church."[6] This sometimes creates an unbiblical balance in a church's leadership and can encourage unhealthy competition between the pastor(s) and the deacons. "This practice is a proven formula for prolonged church warfare.[7] One of the reasons many pastors quit their ministry is because of conflict with deacons. This is not how the deacon ministry was designed.

The reason that the apostles did not take on the responsibility of administrating the distribution of funds to the widows is that they already

---

[3] Stewart Custer, *Witness to Christ: A Commentary on Acts*, (Greenville, SC: Bob Jones University Press, 2000), p. 76.

[4] Alexander Strauch, *Minister of Mercy: the New Testament Deacon*, (Littleton, CO: Lewis and Roth Publishers, 1992), p. 28.

[5] Stewart Custer, *Witness to Christ: A Commentary on Acts*, (Greenville, SC: Bob Jones University Press, 2000), p. 76.

[6] Alexander Strauch, *Minister of Mercy: the New Testament Deacon*, (Littleton, CO: Lewis and Roth Publishers, 1992), p. 9.

[7] Ibid.

had a primary responsibility; to give themselves to prayer and the ministry of the word (v. 4). Thus, the primary responsibility of a deacon is to serve (*diakonos*). There is a difference between overseeing others serving, a pastoral responsibility (*episkopos*), and being the servant. While a deacon is part of the church's leadership, his main duty is serving others.[8] This does not mean that pastors are not to be servants also. Jesus plainly commanded His disciples to serve one another (Jn. 13:12-14). The best kind of pastoral leadership is "servant leadership." "This is the kind of leadership where the God of all power and glory gives His life to save the souls of fallen men who have rejected Him—the kind of leadership that gains by giving, lives by dying, and rises by kneeling."[9] Pastors should be servants, particularly in ways that involve spiritual service such as prayer, discipleship, preaching, and teaching. Deacons are those who come alongside the pastor(s) to aid in the administrative functions of the church. It is not a position of rule. It is not a teaching position. "Thus the work of the deacons, the servant-officers of the church, is to oversee the people's practical, material needs."[10] Though the Bible anticipates that deacons will be spiritual men, their function is to care for the material things of the church as they are led by the pastor(s).[11] Some examples of deacon duties are: maintaining the church facilities, distributing benevolence to the needy, aiding the pastor(s) in administrating the church's finances, helping the congregation as ushers, and leading in various logistical capacities.[12]

---

[8] There is no biblical office of church trustee. Some States such as North Carolina require organized churches to have trustees. Their function is to be officers in the church in a legal capacity. Because this not a biblical office, there are no official qualifications that the individual trustees must meet. Likewise, trustees should not exercise any real oversight or administrative capacities in the day to day operation of the church.

[9] Paul Chappell, *The Spiritual Leader*, (Lancaster, CA: Striving Together Publications, 2008), p. 26.

[10] Alexander Strauch, *Minister of Mercy: the New Testament Deacon*, (Littleton, CO: Lewis and Roth Publishers, 1992), p. 75.

[11] A pastor friend walked into a deacons meeting and told them that he was quitting effective immediately. His announcement created quite a stir. The men were shocked, until he smiled and told them that he was referring to his being a deacon. The pastor had been responsible for cutting the grass at the church and he rightly pointed out to these men that it was really their responsibility.

[12] Benjamin Merkle, "The Biblical Qualification and Responsibilities of Deacons," https://www.9marks.org/article/biblical-qualifications-and-responsibilities-deacons/, accessed May 28, 2019.

The Deacon's Qualifications

Similar to the qualifications for pastors, deacons are to be men of noble character and impeachable conduct. Their spiritual life and testimony should be above reproach. They should be revered for their personal conduct (*semnos*) in at least three ways. (1) They should be revered as someone who does not say one thing to one person and then something else to another (*dilogos—literally, two words*). (2) They should not be men who get drunk (*oino pollo*). (3) They should not serve the Lord in order to enrich themselves (*aischrokerdes*). Rather, they should be known as being faithful in their work for the Lord.[13] Even their family life is important. They should demonstrate moral faithfulness to their wives and lead their families life in a way that brings glory to God and to the testimony of the church (v. 12).[14]

Deacons wives should be known as godly women rejecting both the recreational use of alcohol (*nephalios*) and slander/gossip (*diabolos*). They should be noted for their faithful service to Christ (*pistos*).[15]

The Example of Stephen

One of the men chosen by the Jerusalem church to be a deacon was Stephen, a man who Luke describes as being "full of faith and the Holy Spirit (power)" (Acts 6:5, 8). He performed many signs and wonders Jerusalem (v. 8). There was no way Satan was going to allow him to go unchallenged. He was as influential as Peter and John were when they healed the lame man (chapter 3). Some of the wicked, Greek speaking men in the synagogue debated with him but were unable to "resist the

---

[13] Every man should aspire to be qualified as a deacon in his church, even if he does not hold the office specifically (Tit. 2:2).

[14] V. 12 indicates that they should be husbands (*aner*) to one (*mia*) wife (*gyne*). There is no way to take language literally without reaching the conclusion that the office of deacon, like that of the pastor, is restricted to godly men.

[15] It is likely that the deaconess is not a godly woman who holds the official office of deacon. Rather, she is either the godly wife of a deacon or does the work of a deacon in the local church. See Romans 16:1 for a reference to the godly servant (*diakonos*) Phebe who served in the church in Cenchrea as an example of a deaconess. Every lady in the church should strive to do the work of a deacon (Tit. 2:3-4).

wisdom and spirit by which he spoke" (v. 10). Just as the Sanhedrin hired men to lie about Jesus, they set up false witnesses to lie about Stephen. They accused him of blasphemy, a capital charge in Judaism (v. 13). During the trial, Stephen did not respond in anger to their lies. He sat silently, his face resembling an angel (v. 14).

When he was granted the opportunity to address the Sanhedrin, Stephen preached a powerful sermon detailing how Israel repeatedly rejected God's leader over them. His first example is Joseph, sold into slavery by his brothers (v. 9). His second example is Moses. The people rejected Moses on multiple occasions. They questioned his calling by God to leadership (v. 35). They also rejected his leadership to bring the people into Canaan (v. 39). The people rejected the prophets who called them to only worship Jehovah (v. 52a). Finally, the people, these people, had rejected the greatest prophet, Jesus. They had murdered "the Just One" (v. 52b).

The Sanhedrin did not respond positively to Stephen's sermon like the people did at Pentecost (2:37). They were "pricked" in their heart (*katanyssomai*). The Jewish leaders were "cut" to the heart (*diaprio*). The first is the prick of conviction. The second is the pain of rejection. The Jewish leaders knew they were in the wrong, but were unwilling to admit it. Luke writes that they "gnashed their teeth," an obvious sign of anger at what Stephen said. Stephen was the very opposite of anger. He was filled (*pleres*) with the Spirit. He said to them: "I can see into heaven. Jesus is standing on the right hand of the Father" (v. 56). This sent the Sanhedrin over the edge. They rushed him screaming and holding their ears (v. 57). They threw him over a precipice outside the city gates and stoned him to death (vv. 58-60).

This godly man gave up his life for the cause of Jesus Christ. He is the first Christian martyr. He is also one of the deacons chosen to "wait tables" (6:2). His ministry was not superficial or "beneath him." It was his honor to serve Jesus in this capacity. That he preached this sermon and that it was recorded by Luke and preserved in Scripture is testimony to Stephen's godliness. He is a great example of the kind of man God wants in a deacon for His church.

Deacon Ordination

Godly deacons are a blessing to a church. They are a gift from God just as the pastor is His special gift. In fact, there is no greater blessing to a pastor than godly deacons. Many pastors, particularly younger men, chafe under the leadership of such men. Instead of praising God for their deacons, these pastors think of ways to get around their leadership. This is usually a grand mistake. Effective deacons increase the influence and testimony of a church (Acts 6:7).

There are no official guidelines for how deacons should be selected or ordained to their office. The apostles told the church members to choose godly men to fill the office. After seven men were chosen, a number that probably coincided with the number of Greek speaking believers in the church, the apostles "laid their hands on them" (Acts 6:6). The lack of specificity has caused churches to appoint deacons in different ways. Some put deacon candidates through rigorous ordinations like their pastoral counterparts. Some churches select multiple men and then ask the congregation to choose between them. Some churches appoint deacons to lifetime ministry and others to serve shorter, limited terms. It is a blessing of autonomy of the local church that each can choose their own method for appointing deacons.

Select Godly Men

The biggest obstacle to good deacons in a church is that the men who serve as deacons are not always very good people. Some churches select men to be deacons because they give a lot of money to the church; because they are loud with their opinions; because they are part of a "ruling family" that have been part of the church for many years. Deacons may be opinionate, part of an influential church family, and be great contributors to the offering, but this is no reason to elevate someone to be a deacon. Churches must be diligent to select godly men to the diaconate.

Select Experienced Men

There is a healthy balance between experience and youth. Young men should be encouraged to aspire to be a deacon (as mentioned above). However, immature deacons can seriously hamper the work of God in a church. They can cause trouble with their behavior. Men with life experience who have proven themselves capable are good candidates to be deacons.

Select Faithful Men

Deacons, at least as the New Testament envisions, do not sit in board-rooms making decisions and running the church. They are the people who get their hands dirty. They lead others by example doing some of the most difficult jobs in the church. There is no way someone can be an effective deacon if he has not already demonstrated his faithfulness to the Lord. Deacons should be the kind of people who are in church every time the doors are open. Their lives are examples for others to follow. If a deacon is not faithful, he will not be an effective leader.

Select Reasonable Men

Deacons do make decisions. Just because they are those who "wait tables" (Acts 6:2), they are not without considerable contribution to the direction of the church. Pastors who exclude their deacons from any decision-making are themselves making a big mistake. Deacons often bring years of practical experience into their ministry. Churches should select reasonable men to be deacons. This means that deacons must be willing to work with the pastor(s). At the same time, they should be firm in their convictions. Every experienced pastor can point to times when the deacons saved them from making a ministerial error.

Discipleship Questions

1. Why do pastors and deacons fight? What can be done to alleviate these types of conflicts?

2. What problems can arise from deacons who do not know their biblical responsibilities?

3. Do you think deacons should be ordained?

4. Why is Scripture relatively silent on specifics about the terms deacons fill or how long they should serve?

5. Should every young man seek to be a deacon in the future? Should this be something for which he should strive to become?

Chapter 8

Christian Partnership

O N Thursday, May 31, 2018 the Scripps National Spelling Bee win-
ner, Karthik Nemmani won the yearly contest by correctly spelling the Greek word *koinonia*.[1] While this word is uncommon enough
in the typical American's vocabulary, it should not be unknown to anyone who is a Christian. The word koinonia refers to partnership or
fellowship. It conveys the idea of participating in a joint-venture. For
example, the apostle John writes that we have two levels of Christian
fellowship as a result of our salvation. These two levels are often de-
picted on a graph. We have a vertical fellowship with God and a hor-
izontal fellowship with other believers (1 Jn. 1:3). This relationship is
more than just a casual acquaintance. Our union with God is secured
for us through the indwelling Holy Spirit. Likewise, we have a partnership with other believers in the household of God. Each of us who
were once "not a people," are now part of a specially selected generation, part of the royal priesthood, and a citizen of the heavenly nation
of Christ (1 Pet. 2:9-10). We are all part of the one body in Christ
(as explained in chapter 6). Every believer has a task to fulfill that not
only glorifies God (Matt. 5:16), but is part of his Christian obligation
others.

---

[1] Miller, Ryan. https://www.usatoday.com/story/news/nation/2018/05/31/scripps-national-
spelling-bee-2018-final-round-results-karthik-nemmani/661830002/, accessed March 27, 2019 at
2:09pm.

Interdependence

Christian maturity requires interdependence. This is because God determined it to be so, similar to the way God set the bounds of the physical earth into place. The natural laws of science, which are so important to our everyday existence, were determined by God without any input from man. Likewise, the necessity of interdependence is something which God has established.[2] This need for interdependence is first expressed in Genesis 2:18 where God states that Adam needs a helper fit for him. Without Eve, Adam was incomplete. The way that God has ordained the family is that it is best equipped with both a husband and wife, a dad and mom. Not every family enjoys this structure. Some families, for whatever reason, experience a structure where only one parent is in the home. Single parent homes is not God's ideal for how that family should function.[3]

Likewise, a Christian is supposed to mature and grow in an interdependent environment of his local church. There is no way for this maturity to take place outside the rough and tumble arena of the assembly of Christians. Like a human body, the local church is made up of "body parts." These parts are set into place by God according to His perfect will (Eph. 4:16). Just like a human body has a different systems necessary for proper function, so a church requires each part to be in its proper place functioning according to God's plan. What would you think about a person who had no muscular system, or no skeleton, or was simply missing his skin? That kind of individual would be severely disabled if he was able to live at all.

Moreover, local churches were never intended by God to live independently of one another. The independent church movement, something that is common in America since the early 20th century, is not a spiritually healthy response to the excesses and failures of denominationalism. While denominationalism, at least in the traditional sense,

---

[2] There is a reason why solitary confinement is considered to be a form of torture. God has created man with the need for fellowship with others.

[3] Many times, this is not because someone is at "fault." Sometimes it is because a parent dies while children are still in the home.

is not a biblical system,[4] complete independence is not the right response either.

The way that God created the family, the Christian life, and church life is that each functions best in an interdependent state.[5] This is the way of health that produces maturity. Families can function of sorts without a two-parent home. Christians can have a relationship with Jesus Christ outside of a local church. Churches can live independently of one another. It just is not God's perfect plan that they do so.

Interdependence in the Christian Home

The center of every home should be the Lord Jesus Christ. Ephesians 5:18-6:4 provides a helpful outline for how the Christian home is established. With both parents being "in Christ," each is to be filled with the Spirit (5:18). The control of the Holy Spirit will produce the spiritual qualities upon which a good home is established. These are called "fruits" in Galatians 5:22-23. When the Spirit of God is in control, husbands will love their wives in the same sacrificial manner as Jesus loves the Church. The husband should love his wife as if she was a part of his own body. Paul even states, perhaps a bit strangely, that this kind of love is "self-love" (5:28). The threshold for love within the family is presented simply—a husband must love his wife to the same degree at which he loves himself. Anything less is not Spirit-controlled living and it demonstrates that the husband has not truly crucified his own flesh with its desires and cravings. When this kind of love is not evident in the life of the husband, the marriage will experience conflict. To whatever degree this love is lacking, the conflict may even be explosive.

In the same manner, a Spirit-controlled wife is to be submissive to her husband. She should be ordering her life underneath the will of her

---

[4] As a Baptist, I believe in the Baptist distinctives. One of these is the autonomy of the local church. Interdependence should never overreach so that autonomy within a local church is trampled down.

[5] The progression of these interdependent groups was given to me by Pastor Tim Potter, Grace Church of Mentor, Mentor, Ohio.

husband. This is not a fashionable idea in feminism, even feminism of the evangelical stripe. Biblical headship of the husband is often rejected as antiquated or that Paul was merely expressing cultural ideas of his day that have no bearing on our day. However, a plain reading of the text reveals that God's plan is that wives be submissive to their husbands in the same manner that they are submissive to the Lord. Just as Jesus is the authority of the Church, so a husband is the authority of his wife. This is what the term "head" means.[6]

The key to submission is the phrase "in the Lord" (5:22). The only way that a wife can be truly submissive to her husband is if she submits to him in the same way she submits to Jesus Christ. In other words, she submits to her husband because she is submissive to the Lord.[7] This does not always result in her husband loving her to a greater extent. It would be ideal if that was the case. Yet it does result in her being obedient to the calling of God on her life.

For both the husband and the wife, the concept of love and respect is crucial to the happiness and success of the marriage. As these concepts are put into place the result is the two of them becoming "one." The "one flesh" relationship within marriage illustrates that oneness of the couple. They are no longer two individuals. They are truly one (5:31).

God may choose to bless married couples with children. For those who have not been blessed this way, there are biological and societal pressures which make life difficult. For those who do have children, there are obligations to train and teach those children to order their lives in the Lord. Children are commanded to "obey" their parents. This is also "in the Lord." In the same sense that husbands are to love their wives and wives to reverence their husbands, so parents should love their children and children should reverence their parents. The first commandment with a promised attached, the fifth commandment, is that children "honor" their parents. The fact that the promise

---

[6] Evangelical feminists, often referred to as egalitarians, refuse to accept biblical headship. They interpret the term *head* to mean "source." Just as the head of a river is its source, so the source of a wife is her husband. This is utter non-sense. There is just no way to reconcile that idea that I am the "source" of my wife. She is the product of her parents and in no way connected to me in that sense.

[7] Obviously, submission to Christ takes precedence over submission to any human authority.

is attached is significant.[8] As children living in the home, God expects them to listen and do what their parents command. There is a sense of reasonableness to the command. God does not expect a child to obey any command from a parent to practice immorality. When the child leaves the home, he should show reverence to his parents by listening and heeding their advice. This does not mean that he will necessarily follow every instruction, but it does mean that he should show them honor by listening intently. God gives parents wisdom, even unsaved parents. As parents age, adult children should "honor" their parents by taking care of them as best they can. Honoring one's parents does not end in childhood. It is something that is carried throughout life.

In a home where the husband loves his wife sacrificially, where the wife reverences her husband, and where the children obey and honor their parents, there is a sweet spirit which provides testimony that the Spirit is in control. What Ephesians 5-6 demonstrate is that there is a natural interdependence in a Christian home necessary to the proper functioning of the family.

Interdependence in the local church

Rising up out of the interdependent Christian family is a similar interdependence in the local church. This interdependence is based on the concept of "one another." This comes from the word *allelon*. This term explains the duties of those who are in partnership with each other (*koinonia*). That is, Christians who are in fellowship together have *a divine obligation* to each other. There are no "lone cowboy" Christians who are also obedient to God's Word. It is literally impossible to be obedient to Scripture and go it alone.[9] Not only do each of us need

---

[8] The promise to Israel is that if they honored their parents they were likely to dwell long in the Land of Promise. Five times in Deuteronomy 5-6 Moses states that the necessity of obedience to parents in keeping God's covenant was key to the people prospering in the land. This land was promised to them through Abraham. Paul's use of this promise does not related to a land or even to longevity. Ephesians 6:3 is restating what God promised in Deuteronomy 5-6. Christians have no such promise. We do not expect to inherit a land like Israel does. Rather, the promise in Ephesians 6:3 is a reminder of how important God takes the issue of obedience.
[9] It is imperative that Christians do not become so individualistic that they treat the church as a kind of spiritual smorgasbord where they take some things and leave others. This "take-it-or-leave-it" mentality is ruining the concept of interdependent partnership in local churches and stifling authentic spiritual growth.

others to help us in our Christian walk, we need to help others ourselves. This is why the discipleship culture is so important to a church. The first time "one another" is used in the sense of a Christian community is in John 13:14. In this verse Jesus instructs the disciples to wash each other's feet. Other uses of *allelon* as it relates to community life within a church are as follows:

- John 13:35—Christians should love each other as this is visible evidence of discipleship.

- John 15:12, 17—Jesus commands believers to love each other.

- Romans 12:5—Christians are part of the "one body" of Jesus.

- Romans 12:10—Christians should honor and prefer others before themselves.

- Romans 12:16—Christians should consider each other to care for them.

- Romans 13:8—Christians should love one another.

- Romans 14:13 (used in a negative sense)—Christians should stop judging each other.

- Romans 14:19—Christians should build up each other.

- Romans 15:5—Christians should think about each other (with the idea of offering help).

- Romans 15:7—Christians should receive each other.

- Romans 15:14—Christians should admonish and encourage each other in the Lord.

- Romans 16:16—Christians should greet each other in the Lord (2 Cor. 13:12).

- 1 Corinthians 11:33—Christians should care for each other.

- 1 Corinthians 12:25—Christians should care for each other.

- Galatians 5:13—Christians should serve each other.

- Galatians 5:15 (used in a negative sense)—Christians should be careful not to harm other believers.

- Galatians 5:26 (used in a negative sense)—Christians should not envy or provoke each other.

- Galatians 6:2—Christians should seek to restore those who have been broken by sin.

- Ephesians 4:2—Christians should forebear with each other.

- Ephesians 4:25—Christians should tell the truth to each other.

- Ephesians 5:21—Christians should submit to each other.

- Philippians 2:3—Christians should put others higher than themselves.

- Colossians 3:9—Christians should not lie to each other.

- Colossians 3:13—Christians should forebear and forgive each other.

- 1 Thessalonians 3:12—Christians should abound in love for each other (also 4:9).

- 1 Thessalonians 4:18, 5:11—Christians should comfort each other.

- 1 Thessalonians 5:15—Christians should not return evil for evil to anyone.

- 2 Thessalonians 1:3—Christians should love each other.

- Hebrews 10:24—Christians should encourage each other spiritually.

- James 4:11 (also used in a negative sense)—Christians should not speak ill of others.

- James 5:16—Christians should confess their faults to each other.

- 1 Peter 1:22—Christians should love one another.

- 1 Peter 4:9—Christians should be hospitable to each other.

- 1 Peter 5:5—Christians should be in mutual submission to each other.

- 1 Peter 5:14—Christians should greet each other in the Lord.

- 1 John 1:7—Christians should have koinonia with each other.

- 1 John 3:11, 23, 4:7, 11—Christians should love each other.

- 2 John 5— Christians should love each other.

Interdependence among churches

Jesus prayed to the Father that the church would be unified. His prayer was specifically for those who believe in Him on the basis of the testimony of the apostles (Jn. 17:20). "That they all may be one" (v. 21).

This prayer indicates what is already spiritually true, but is, unfortunately, not always practically true.[10] The unity for which Jesus prays, moreover, is based upon His own relationship with the Father.[11] This is the essence of 1 John 1:7. Ordering one's life in the light (life) of Jesus through His gospel is the basis of all Christian fellowship. It is the reason why someone who professes to being in Christ but hates his brother is actually in darkness (death) (2:9). Such an individual does not have eternal life in him (3:15).

This unity is also expressed in the way the church is described as a bride of Christ. It is not brides, plural, but bride, singular. She is the Lamb's wife (Rev. 21:9). Jesus gave Himself for His bride, the Church, in order to present it to Himself as a glorious Church having not defect (Eph. 5:25-27). Some read these passages as depicting something in the future. Clearly, there is an eschatological component to these verses. However, it is short-sighted to see all unity among believers as only reserved for future times.[12] If the Church were everything the Lord wants it to be right now, it would have some interdependence to it. "The image of the church as the bride of Christ likewise argues for unity among believers."[13]

The practical result of this intended unity is that the burden or weight should be on unity among believers, not on separation. While ecclesiastical separation is one of the distinctives of the Baptists,[14] it should not be our natural state. Ecclesiastical separation should be a last resort after all efforts of unity are exhausted. There are pastors and churches that separate over everything. They argue that "a church or religious organization must be in absolute or near absolute agreement with another church or religious organization or must belong to the right association or denomination for there to be any fellowship."[15] This is

---

[10] The verbs in John 17:21 are in the subjunctive mood indicating the purpose or result of what is occurring.

[11] Millard Erickson, *Christian Theology*, (Grand Rapids: Baker Books, 2004), p. 1137.

[12] For a comprehensive discussion on the Church as the Bride, see Earl Radmacher, *The Nature of the Church*, (Portland: Western Baptist Press, 1972), pp. 241-246.

[13] Erickson, 1138.

[14] See https://www.mbu.edu/seminary/the-logic-of-brapsis/, accessed May 23, 2019.

[15] Larry Oats, *Dispensationalism: A Basis for Ecclesiastical Separation*, (Watertown, WI: Maranatha Baptist Press, 2013), KL 13.

not what Jesus' High Priestly prayer is indicating as the ideal. There should, at the very least, be some willingness to conciliar unity among all believers that does not violate the autonomy of the local church and the problem of ecumenicalism. No church should join together with a church that espouses doctrines that are unbiblical, or worse, antithetical to the gospel. Likewise, no church should be so unwilling to cooperate with another that there is a kind of spiritual isolation that develops. Pastors should pray and fellowship with other pastors whenever possible. Wherever opportunities for cooperation exist, churches should join together for the cause of Christ. Missions is a great example of this. Many churches are incapable of providing all the support for a missionary so churches join together to provide that support.

Does Not the Spirit Indwell?

Christian partnership is evident in the way Paul describes the church plant in Corinth. Leaving Athens, Paul traveled to Corinth where he met Acquila and Priscilla, a Jewish couple whose occupation was tentmaking (Acts 18:2). They had recently relocated to Corinth from Italy because Claudius Caesar had expelled all the Jews from Rome. Paul apparently led them to faith in Jesus because when Apollos came across them later on, they helped him understand the gospel better than he did (v. 26).

In Corinth, Paul preached in the synagogue every sabbath day preaching Jesus to the Jews and Greek proselytes (v. 4). Because the Jews resisted the gospel, Paul relocated to the house of Justus, a Gentile (v. 7). For 18 months Paul preached the Scriptures to the newly established church of Corinth.

When Paul later describes this time, he refers to the church in two ways. The church is a farm (1 Cor. 3:6) and a building (v. 10). He planted the seeds. Apollos worked in the farm. God grew the crops. Likewise, he laid the foundation (v. 10), and others built on that foundation. To this Paul adds: "Do you not know that the Spirit of God indwells you?" (v. 16).

It is imperative that churches recognize that every true church where the gospel is preached and where the Scriptures are honored, though imperfect, the Spirit indwells. Corinth had major problems. There were immoral people in the church. There were fractious people there. Many were still spiritual babies (3:3). But the Spirit of God indwelt them. Wherever the Spirit of God is, there should also be unity. Other believers are our partners. Whenever possible, Christians should partner together interdependently to increase the testimony of Jesus in the world.

Discipleship Questions

1. Why is it important that Christian families demonstrate interdependence?

2. Looking at the list of "one-anothers," which of these is most difficult for you?

3. In what ways can churches become more interdependent?

4. Why is a critical spirit of other pastors, believers, or churches a violation of interdependence?

Chapter 9

The Discipleship Culture

S ANCTIFICATION is one of the most important aspects of the Christian life and involves radical change on the personal level. This is generally understood by theologians as the doctrine of sanctification. Followers of Jesus Christ should mature in their faith and see a change in lifestyle as they become more like Him. The Apostle Paul wrote that saved people are a new creation in Christ. The old way of life is gone and a new way of life has taken its place (2 Cor. 5:17). Those who were dead in sin have been made alive in Jesus, kind of like a "before and after" picture (Eph. 2:1-10). Where once an unsaved person who ordered his life as he wanted (really according to his flesh, the world, and ultimately Satan), now he orders his life in the Spirit doing what God wants (Rom. 8:1-4). He no longer submits himself to the mold of the world, to be pressed into a shape that is displeasing to God. Instead, he is transformed from the inside-out submitting his life as worship to God (Rom. 12:1-2). He may still follow his sinful lusts from time to time, but as he matures in his walk with Jesus, his life bears Spirit-fruit and not flesh-fruit (Gal. 5:16-25).

Whether one knows this or not, this is the discipleship process. Disciples are simply followers of Jesus Christ. It is impossible to be a Christian and not a disciple. Christians manifest their discipleship in three distinct ways: by identifying with Jesus, by conforming their behavior and attitudes to reflect Jesus' own character and conduct, and by living out the commission to Jesus to make disciples themselves. Every church should be committed to the discipleship culture. It should be convinced that discipleship is important and that disciples are made through the work of a local church. This is how the New Testament presents the discipleship culture to the church.

The Titus Model

The book of Titus is presented last among the pastoral epistles of Paul.[1] It provides a very helpful example of how the discipleship culture should be active in every church. The book begins by identifying its author, Paul, and its recipient, Titus (1:1-4). Immediately after the introduction, Paul indicates that he *purposefully* left Titus in Crete with a specific task. Their missions work together ended incomplete, before the churches on the island were fully established. Paul instructed Titus to complete the work in Crete. Think about that. For some unknown reason, Paul left the work unfinished. Outside of reasons of persecution, Paul is always a "finisher." It is tempting to think the that only way for completion of the mission would be for Paul to return and finish what he started. He did not do that. Instead, Paul entrusted Titus with the responsibility to finish the job of organizing the churches on the island (v. 5). This task had two parts. First, Titus was to set in order the things that were wanting. Second, he was to ordain elders in every city.[2]

The Emphasis on Discipleship

While there may not be one central theme of the book of Titus, it is apparent that discipleship is a major one. Paul clearly states that Titus was to be involved in making disciples on Crete. The process was a simple one. The doctrines of Paul transferred to Titus. He was to transfer them to the disciples in Crete. Paul indicates that the church is where there is a continual transfer of authority from one generation

---

[1] It is listed last in the Canon, but it was probably written before 2 Timothy.

[2] Apparently, there were literally hundreds of cities on the island and each would need to be evangelized. The churches planted in each city would need organization. This was Titus' task. See William Barclay, "The Letters of Timothy, Titus, and Philemon," *The New Daily Bible Study*, p. 263.

of leaders to the next. "Paul cautions mature believers never to act as though they are only responsible for themselves. The knowledge that Christian maturity brings, combined with the spiritual dangers that others face, obligate Christian leaders to lead."[3]

The apostle outlined two basic methods for Titus to accomplish this two-pronged task. The first method was preaching. Titus was to faithfully preach God's Word in the Cretan churches. He was to "rebuke them sharply in order that they would be sound in the faith" (v. 13).[4] The second method was discipleship. Of the two methods, moreover, the emphasis in Titus is on the second. Discipleship was the primary means by which Titus would accomplish his mission.

First, discipleship was the means through which pastors would be identified and authorized to lead the Cretan churches. It is evident from the introduction that this is how Paul had identified and authorized Titus. He refers to Titus as "his own son after the common faith" (v. 4). This kinship was not by blood, at least not by Paul's blood. The relationship was based upon their mutual submission to the gospel of Jesus and by Paul's training Titus as a younger man in vocational ministry. Thus, a transfer had already taken place where Paul discipled Titus (much like he did with Timothy) training him for this ministry. There is a sense here of both personal investment in Titus and trust that Titus would follow through on God's leading in his life. For the Christians in Crete, Titus, not Paul, was the man of the hour. This was only possible because Paul had already discipled Titus.

Consequently, necessity dictated that Titus reproduce himself in others just as Paul had done in him. While the details of this discipleship relationship is not given, it is obvious that they spent a lot of time working side-by-side. At the very least, they had been together in ministry on Crete. It seems undeniable that Paul used this time to not only begin the process of church planting on Crete but also the process of discipleship of Titus. It is impossible to determine which work was more important from the other.

---

[3] Chapell, Bryan. "1 & 2 Timothy and Titus," *Preaching the Word Commentary Series*, p. 292.

[4] This rebuke (*elegcho*) means to convict or convince. Sometimes it involves correction. This is the word Paul uses in 2 Timothy 3:16 as one of the activities of the Scripture translated "reproof."

The Process of Discipleship

The stress in discipleship is on the spoken truth. Specifically, Titus was to speak "the things which become sound doctrine" (2:1). His ministry was directed toward three groups of people. First, Titus was to have a ministry among the older men in the church. He was to instruct them in God's truth so that they would mature in their faith. The result of sound doctrine being conveyed is Christian maturity. The list Paul gives of the results is amazing. Sound doctrine leads to sobriety (abstinence from the recreational use of alcohol *or at least drunkenness*);[5] to a lifestyle that is honorable; to a grounded faith that is not easily shaken; to God-like love for others; and to endurance even during the worst trials (2:2). These qualities are evidence of godliness much like faith, hope, and love are obvious Christian virtues. In fact, they seem to be linked together.[6]

He was also to have a ministry to the older women in the church. The result of Titus' discipleship among the women was a holy demeanor. Such a spirit would result in restraint. They would not be gossips spreading slander around the church and they would be restrained in their use of alcohol. On the other side, their holy demeanor would make them able to teach others what is good. Specifically, this teaching ministry was to the younger women. Of the four groups in the church, older men and women along with younger men and women, Titus was not directed to disciple the younger women.[7] This is where the discipleship culture is most evident. Titus' teaching the older women had a direct impact on the younger women. This is just like the benefit of Paul's ministry to the Cretans through Titus. The younger women benefitted from Titus' ministry to the older women. In fact, the entire discipleship chain looks something like this: Jesus à Paul à Titus à Older Women à Younger Women à Children (though unmentioned,

---

[5] Drunkeness was a major problem in the ancient world where there was not always the availability of clean drinking water. Wine (*oinos*) was used medicinally in order to prevent stomach disorders and promote good health. See 1 Timothy 5:23.

[6] Litfin, A. Duane, "Titus," *The Bible Knowledge Commentary*, p. 764.

[7] There is probably a practical reason for this as the older women were in a better position to teach their younger counterparts. See Hayne Griffin, "1, 2 Timothy Titus," *The New American Commentary*, Vol. 34. p. 300.

there is an obvious inference here). There are four stages of separation from Jesus' ministry to Paul to the young wives ministry to their children. This is one of the reasons why discipleship is so important in a church. Specifically, the older women with a holy demeanor were to train the younger women to be moderate and sensible, to love their husbands and children, to be self-controlled curbing their appetites,[8] to be modest in moral purity, to be domestically inclined, and to be submissive to their husbands. The result of such behavior was a good Christian testimony.[9]

Finally, Titus was to come alongside (*parakaleo*) the younger men in the same manner as the Holy Spirit comes alongside the individual believer (2:6). The manner of this exhortation lends itself to discipleship. His words were to be supported by an exemplary lifestyle. Everything he said had to be combined with an excellent testimony (vv. 7-8). Specifically, he was to encourage the young men to be self-controlled. This may be the most important quality in a young Christian man. The "sins of youth" are often the result of a lack of self-discipline or moral restraint. While preaching and teaching in a church is beneficial to new or immature saints, the greatest influence on them should be from an individual discipler. This may be his father if he is a Christian, but it also includes the ministry of other church men who exemplify personal self-discipline in all areas of life. Thus, the best life lessons are often more "caught" than "taught."[10]

---

[8] This is a reference to the lower passions often referred to in Scripture by the bodily location of the belly.

[9] Some scholars believe that the restrictions on the young wives is best understood against the backdrop of Greek society where women seldom left the home for any reason. They argue that these commands are therefore temporary. However, even if there is a cultural application that Paul is making, the overall argument still stands. Younger women should deport themselves in their own culture in ways that bring praise upon their Christian faith, not disrepute. It is the responsibility of the older women in the church to disciple the younger women to conduct their affairs this way. See Bryan Chapell, "1 & 2 Timothy and Titus," *Preaching the Word Commentary Series*, p. 330.

[10] There is a fourth group mentioned in Titus 2. Paul refers to Titus' ministry among the slaves. Slavery was part of the Greek and Roman society. Slaves typically had very few if any personal rights. At the same time, many slaves came to Christ and formed a large portion of the early church. Onesimus, according to some ancient documents, was a pastor even though he was a slave to Philemon. Titus was to instruct them to be obedient to their masters and to work hard (2:9-10).

The Discipleship Message

The message that Titus was to preach centered on Jesus, flowing out of the gospel message itself (v. 11) and its applications to the believer's life. The grace of God teaches that Christians should "say no" to sin (ungodliness and worldly lust) and live a lifestyle characterized by self-control (a repetitive theme in this section) and personal righteousness and piety. Moreover, the focus on Jesus was fixed on the believer's hope in His "glorious appearing" when our Lord returns to earth to establish His kingdom (2:13). The immediate consequence of this doctrine is that because Jesus gave up Himself for us, He redeemed us from a life of sin (v. 14). In other words, Christians should work hard to bring glory to God.

Paul makes a contrast here over what the good works will do in one's personal life. Positively, a Christian should be submissive to human authorities that God has set up (3:1). They should not be aggressively confrontational or argumentative with others but demonstrate a spiritual meekness and humility in dealing with other people (v. 2). Negatively, a Christian should not live as he once did when apart from God's grace in Christ. He should demonstrate a lack of God's wisdom by being disobedient to his authorities, being led away from godliness by his own sinful desires. He should not be controlled by anger toward others, envy of their well-being, or hating them (v. 3). That is not in keeping with God's love and kindness toward believers (v. 4). In fact, one's salvation is not according to good works at all. Rather, it is God's love motivated grace that offers salvation (v. 5). This has been "shed abundantly" on every Christian. This same loving and gracious spirit should be evident in every Christian's life. The most valuable member of a community should be a Christian (v. 8).

Discipleship Success and Failure

Paul's expectation of Titus is that he will be successful in organizing the churches on Crete by instilling a discipleship culture within each congregation. Unfortunately, not everyone would be interested in the discipleship culture. Paul warns that some are interested in the minutia of non-doctrinal matters; things that do not really matter or have no direct bearing on the Christian life (v. 9). Instead of encouraging unity and grace in the body of Christ, such matters divide believers from one another. Paul refers to these as stupid issues such as a controversies over genealogies or even Old Testament law. These arguments are harmful to the church and should be avoided.

For those who refuse to stand apart from such debates (*peristemi*), they should be admonished (counseled) a couple of times and then set apart themselves from church membership (v. 10). Divisive issues are that dangerous. When an individual church member refuses to submit himself to church leadership on these matters, he must be put out of the church.

Transformed

Transformation is the purpose of discipleship. God's goal is for all people of all nations throughout time should turn from worshipping idols or themselves to worshipping Jesus who has given Himself in order to redeem mankind.[11] The process of this transformation is sanctification. No Christian learns Christian maturity in a vacuum. Every Christian needs someone to come alongside him and teach him how to read God's Word, how to interact with other believers, how to lead others to Christ, and how to lead those who come to Christ into a life of discipleship.[12] This is God-honoring transformation.

Discipleship Questions

1. What is the goal of discipleship?

2. In what ways is discipleship different from just attending church?

3. What practical wisdom does Paul reveal by preventing Titus from discipling "the younger women?" Whose responsibility is that?

---

[11] Colin Marshall and Tony Payne, *The Vine Project*, (Waterloo, Australia: Matthias Media, 2016), KL 2133.

[12] Tim Potter at Grace Church of Mentor teaches it this way: "Each one reach one; each one teach one; each one be taught by one; for life."

4. Are you presently in a discipleship relationship with someone else?

Chapter 10

God's Call to Christian Service

THE game is called tug-of-war. It is a very simple game. It's played with two teams and one rope. There are almost no rules and the game requires only a few instructions. Each player picks up the rope and pulls. That's it. There is nothing else to know. There is no game box with a complex series of "if this happens . . . then do this." There is none of that. There are only three necessary components—weight, brute strength, and teamwork. While the first two might seem most important, it is teamwork that determines the outcome. The tug-of-war team where everyone pulls together usually wins. The team that struggles to work together usually loses. There is no one player who determines the outcome by his own athletic talent or sheer force of will. There are no Michael Jordan's or Tom Brady's in tug-of-war. There is no GOAT (greatest of all time). The game is based on everyone pulling together.

It is the same for an effective church. There is something terribly wrong in a church where the pastors and other leaders do most of the ministry. God's plan for His church is that *every* member is actively engaged in the Lord's work.[1] That includes the children of the church. Think of how valuable Paul's nephew was to his ministry in Jerusalem (Acts 23:12-21). His intervention in the plot to kill Paul was instrumental in his being rescued by the Roman soldiers from the band of

---

[1] This was one of the themes repeated often by Bud Calvert during his pastoral ministry at Fairfax Baptist Temple, Fairfax, VA.

murderous Jews. Everyone in a church is important. God desires everyone to be invested fully in the church. Everyone is called to ministry. Some serve God vocationally (as an occupation) and others as part of their service to Him. Both are equally important. If the vocational "ministers" are the only one's serving, the church will begin to lose its effectiveness. Every church member should be using the gifts of the Spirit that have been given him in ministry to God in the context of his local church. In this sense, there is no value of one member above another. Each is equally important for the proper functioning of the church.

The Human Body

In stressing the necessity of unity within the church, the apostle Paul explained to the Corinthians that every church functions like a human body (1 Cor. 12:12). As explained in chapter 2, while the church is a singular whole, it is made up of many parts. There is an organic connection between each individual member. The body has hands and feet (v. 15). It has ears and eyes (v. 16). Each church member has a functional responsibility in the church just like each body part is important. Every congregation should have both diversity and unity. The diversity is in the multiplicity of gifts in the membership. The unity is how these gifts operate together.

Think about a baseball pitcher standing on the mound, one run ahead in the 7th game of the World Series. The bases are loaded and there are two outs. The opposing team has their best player at the plate. For the next few minutes, millions of people are focused on an exchange between two individuals. They stand there about 60 feet apart. Both teams have played over two hundred games since the beginning of spring training. It all comes down to this. The pitcher is the first to move. He goes into his wind-up. His body weight shifts. His nervous system fires various signals to his brain from his hand holding to ball and from his legs as they move in unison. His hips and shoulders turn. Everything is directed at the precise moment when the ball will leave his hands rolling across his fingers. If he throws a perfect pitch, he may strike out the batter and his team will win the Series. If he throws a bad pitch, the batter might just win the game for his team. If he is to be successful, the pitcher's entire body has to work as one. In a split second, the ball arrives at home plate and the batter's body goes through a similar process.

The church is just like that pitcher and batter. The church is a body similar to a human body. "It takes up many members to make up a body. Inevitably, the members differ, but their differences do not affect the fact that there is a fundamental unity."[2] If the pitcher's hand refuses to release the ball, he commits a "balk" and the runner at third base will walk home winning the game. If the batter's arms refuse to swing (if the pitch is a strike), he is in jeopardy of being called out on strikes and his team will lose the game. Their body parts have to work or everything may be lost. "Therefore individual members cannot contract out." Every body part has to work for the outcome to be successful.

What if the pitcher's body was just one big eyeball? What would that look like? How would he even get to the pitcher's mound, by rolling out across the infield? Paul writes that if the whole body was just an eye, it would not be able hear anything. Without ears, there is no way to hear (v. 17). The truth is, God has deliberately placed each person in the church and specifically gifted each for service to the whole. "It is not just arrangement; God created the parts to make a body like this . . . He made them all just as He wanted them to be."[3] Every person in the church is necessary. Soldiers severely injured in battle sometimes sacrifice parts of their bodies, a debt that our nation cannot possibly repay to them. They lose a leg or a hand and that loss is real. Try buttoning a shirt with only one hand. See how hard it is to carry groceries using only one leg. Likewise, every church member is an important part of the body. "They are indispensable. The body cannot do without them."[4] No one is going to pitch game 7 of the World Series without working arms or legs. No church is going to be effective without every member actively engaged in God's work.

---

[2] Morris, Leon, "1 Corinthians," *Tyndale New Testament Commentaries*, 170.
[3] Ibid, 172.
[4] Ibid, 173.

Essential Growing

The first obligation of the individual saint is to grow spiritually. Immature believers are a danger to themselves and possibly to the church of which they are a part. They are susceptible to being "carried about with every wind of doctrine" (Eph. 4:14). Like a ship that is adrift on the ocean during a storm, they are tossed around (*peripheromenoi*). The imagery is of a spinning top that rotate with a dizzying effect.[5] Those who are confusing these immature saints are false teachers whose method is to deceive like a card sharp who uses sleight of hand to trick the other players at the table and cheat them in the game.

This does not mean that immature believers should be shunned or cast out of the church. On the contrary, it is the obligation of mature believers to speak the truth to them in love (v. 15). "This fundamental concern for the truth is the secret of maturity in the church."[6] It is likely that Paul is referring to the importance of discipling those who are new in the faith by teaching them "line upon line, and precept upon precept." Spiritual growth is the result of God's Spirit using His Word to train up His children to be like His Son. "Where the 'word of truth' is taught and believed, it bears fruit."[7] Thus, it is the obligation of mature saints to train up immature saints by instructing them in God's Word. The Scriptures are useful and beneficial to teach spiritual truth (2 Tim. 3:16). The Bible is the center of biblical training.[8] Through training, the child becomes a man, he measures up to the stature of the fulness of Christ (Eph. 4:13). In the Scriptures, he is convicted in areas of life where he falls short of the perfect example of Jesus. A right response to this reproof is biblical change. Like a group of tourists traveling through a big city, it is easy to get lost without a guide. The guide keeps you on the right course, heading the right direction. When Christians get off track, the Scriptures help bring a course correction. Galatians 6:1, along with Ephesians 4:15 indicate that mature saints

---

[5] A. Skevington Wood, "Ephesians," *The Expositor's Bible Commentary*, Vol. 11, p. 59.
[6] Ibid, p. 59.
[7] Colin Marshall and Tony Payne, *Trellis and the Vine*, Kindle Location 1003.
[8] Ibid, KL 871.

are also involved in helping erring believers back onto the right track. More than any other activity in the church, this is what the New Testament explains is the calling of every church member.

Effectual Working

When a car stops working, a mechanic gets under the hood to diagnose the problem. His purpose is to get the car operating as it should. A good mechanic has years of experience working with cars and has expert knowledge of the manufacturers specifications for each part of the car. By looking at the car on this level, he can figure out why the car isn't running right and make the necessary repairs. The anticipated result is that the car owner is pleased to find that his broken car is fixed and he can drive it home. When a church is operating as it should, every part of the whole is working in tandem with each other. Going back to the body metaphor, the church should be like a body where the joints are not out of socket, a painful injury. Each body part should be put together correctly so that the body can coalesce around what it is supposed to be doing. If one part of the body is not functioning right, medication or even surgery may be required. Think of what it would be like to have a stomach that just decided to stop working. Just like a car that is running on all cylinders, so every individual body part works together in harmony in order for the body to function as it should (Eph. 4:16).

Love

Love is what makes everything work. The apostle Paul hints at this at the beginning of Ephesians 4. Every church member is to embrace the calling to which he was called. That is, every Christian should be actively involved in God's work. Because of the intimacy of the body parts being interconnected, this anticipates that Christians rub up against each other frequently. Consequently, the essential growth and effectual work of each believer in the church requires a corresponding atti-

tude of personal humility, a profound sense of one's relative unimportance, gentleness, and patience with others. These qualities together
allow for church members to withstand each other's faults. Love is the
center of all of this. Mature saints instruct younger believers by speaking the truth "in love" (Eph. 4:15). The individual body parts are able
to work together because they love the other parts of the body (v. 16).

This love does not allow any room for lying. A Christian who lies
to other believers is not acting out of Christ-like love (v. 25). The saint
who loses his temper with another is not expressing himself in love
(v. 26). You cannot steal from someone you love (v. 28). It is strange
for someone to speak rotten words to another person that he loves (v.
29). People who love are, by nature, forgiving people (v. 32). This kind
of love, above all other qualities and traits, is that which testifies to a
person's Christ-likeness (5:1-2).

A believer who loves never gets selfishly angry with others but is
kind (1 Cor. 13:4). He is not jealous or envious of others when things
to well for them. He does not brag about himself (or his family) in
such a way that puts others down. A loving Christian is not rude or
self-serving. He does not get provoked by the failures of others, even
when those failures impact him. He does not expect the worst out of
others (v. 5). He does not get happy when others fail, but likewise, he
does not ignore those failures at the expense of the truth (v. 6). He puts
up with other people. He hopes the best for them. He believes that
God will mature them in His time. He remains this way, even when
others might encourage him to give up on a difficult fellow believer (v.
7). Finally, a Christian who loves never stops loving (v. 8).

Pull the Rope

Every Christian should be pulling the rope of ministry. This will not
ever mean the exact same thing for any two Christians in church. We
are not the same. We do not have the same gifts and do not have
the same level of experience and maturity. Regardless, we should all
be focused on pulling the same rope. "Simply by virtue of being a

disciple of Jesus and filled with the Holy Spirit...all Christians have the privilege, the joy, and responsibility of being involved in the work God is doing in our world, the 'work of the Lord.'"[9]

Discipleship Questions

1. Why is it important for every Christian to be actively involved in God's work?

2. What is the problem with a church that elevates one spiritual gift over the others?

3. How many ministries in a church should an individual church member have? Is there a limit? Should there be?

4. Why do you think love is so important for Christian service?

---

[9] Ibid, KL 587.

Chapter 11

Accountability

IN 2005, a large church in the upper Midwest went through a well-publicized crisis over the importance of church membership.[1] Their difficulty centered on what to do with those who attended the church faithfully, but were not convinced on the doctrine of believers baptism. These were people who held to a position of infant baptism that is more common in Presbyterianism. This was not an unimportant question. What makes someone a church member and how is that individual accountable to the church? One of the ways the pastor addressed the issue was to preach a series of sermons on church membership. While rarely the subject of a sermon series in today's church, accountability between church members is not a minor doctrine. It is primary in terms of Baptist ecclesiology. Church members voluntarily submit themselves to the whole, acknowledging that there is mutual accountability between them for each other. This includes everyone, even the pastor and his family. Each individual member of a church is responsible to the others for what he believes and how he conducts his life.

Concern for the Spiritual Life of One Another

Accountability arises from the natural concern that believers should have for one another, particularly regarding the spiritual life of indi-

---

[1] Bethlehem Baptist Church in Minneapolis, Minnesota.

vidual members.[2] In Galatians 6 for example, the admonition from the apostle Paul is for Christians to demonstrate their love for others through personal confrontation (Gal. 6:1).[3] Those who were spiritual, that is Spirit-controlled, were to restore those who were spiritually hurting for the purpose of restoring them to usefulness for Jesus. This confrontation was the result of loving service to each other (Gal. 5:13). Refusing to confront a brother or sister who was struggling with sin was tantamount to denying the second command in the law, to love one's neighbor as himself (v. 14). The temptation is, when someone is erring spiritually, to observe the sin and then mention it to others. This is really little better than pure gossip and not what God intends for His church. Paul calls this kind of response "biting" and "devouring" (v. 15). Note the use of the mouth in such action. Rather, believers are to walk in the Spirit (v. 16) and produce fruits of the Spirit (vv. 22-23). Love is the first of these fruits. Moreover, this Spirit-enabled love requires holding a fellow Christian accountable when he is struggling with sin. This is what it means to bear the burdens of each other (Gal. 6:2). This is what it means to fulfill the law of Christ (John 15:12).

Such concern requires two additional things. First, confronting a fellow believer who is spiritually struggling requires a commitment to humility. The believers in Corinth should have been sorrowing over the sin of their professed "brother" who was living in immorality (1 Cor. 5:2). This confession includes acknowledging the spiritual guilt of the member in a manner similar to Daniel (Dan. 9) and Nehemiah (Neh. 1). Both confess the sin of the people before the Lord. Daniel prayed that the people had sinned by failing to keep the covenant (Dan. 9:4-5), and by refusing to listen to God's prophets (v. 6). Nehemiah prayed in a similar fashion acknowledging that he had sinned along with his father's house (Neh. 1:6). He confesses that they did not keep

---

[2] One of the ways that the Bible describes a church is that it is a family. Family members should naturally care for one another.

[3] Some believers take confrontation to the extreme by confronting people over trivial matters. That is not to say that sin is trivial, but that confrontation as described in Galatians 6 is over more life-dominating sins. If Christians were to confront each other over every sin observed, there would be no time in the day left for anything else. Moreover, believers are told to forebear one another which implies a sort of threshold before confrontation takes place.

God's commands given by Moses (v. 10). It also includes a kind of humility that recognizes that the sin of another is a sin that anyone is capable of committing. At the moment of holding another accountable for sin is not the time to be arrogantly asserting (or even thinking) that his sin is outside the realm of your own personal behavior.[4] Only unbelievers claim to be free from sin or to have never sinned (1 Jn. 1:8, 10). Christians, particularly those in the process of holding another believer accountable for sin, must recall the promise that God gives grace to the humble, promising to lift them up (Ja. 4:6, 10).

Second, confrontation over sin requires a willingness to forgive those who acknowledge their sin and turn from it in repentance. Paul refers to this specifically in 2 Corinthians 2:4. Some believe that there is a lost letter from Paul to the Corinthians that is titled "The Painful Letter." This letter followed a visit that occurred after 1 Corinthians was written but before 2 Corinthians.[5] Almost nothing is known about this situation that caused this visit. Apparently, there were people in the Corinthian church who were disparaging Paul and questioning his spiritual authority. The letter had its intended effect. Many of the Corinthians responded to Paul's letter positively, and the result was that one of the offending members was punished. This caused the man great personal grief and it is likely that he repented of his sin. Paul's counsel to the Corinthians is to restore the man to fellowship because of his repentance (2 Cor. 2:6-10). They were to confirm their love to the man and forgive him.

The Mending Process

The purpose of spiritual confrontation is to restore (*kataritzo*) the offending church member back to full fellowship within the church. The word restore means to mend something broken or to repair it. Paul the tent-maker reaches into some of the vocabulary from his secular profession to explain how believers should react to repenting saints.

---

[4] See the quotation by Bob Jones, Sr. "Any sin that any sinner ever committed, every sinner under proper provocation could commit." https://www.goodreads.com/quotes/1039609-any-sin-that-any-sinner-ever-committed-every-sinner-under, accessed May 14, 2019.

[5] Murry J. Harris, "2 Corinthians," *The Expositor's Bible Commentary*, Vol. 10. p. 308.

Another way to think about restoration is like a doctor setting a broken bone putting it back into place.[6] This should be done as gently as possible. There is no room for purposefully embarrassing someone in the goal of demonstrating a strong stance against sin.

Once the sinning saint has repented, church leaders should encourage the church to pray for him as he begins taking new steps forward in Christian discipleship (Ja. 5:10). The forgiven member should be restored to full-fellowship within the body and opportunities for Christian service should begin to open themselves to him again. The point of the mending process is to restore the sinning/forgiven saint back to spiritual usefulness, not to permanently set him aside.[7]

Categories of Accountability

Some believers think of everyone else's business as their own. These spiritual busybodies enjoy confronting others over trivial matters. While they justify their actions as necessary for the purity of the church, they are really just nosey-britches inserting themselves unnecessarily into the lives of other people.[8] This is not what God intends for accountability in the church.

Unity. The first category of accountability is unity. Disunity is one of the most destructive forces that Satan can unleash upon a church. If he can divide God's people from one another, he can diminish or even eliminate their testimony for Christ in a community. Disunity comes from a couple of different places. First, it can be the result of interpersonal conflict. Jesus warns against this type of disunity (Matt. 18:15-17). He gives a process believers should follow when addressing interpersonal conflict with each other. All conflict should be resolved,

---

[6] James M. Boice, "Galatians," *The Expositor's Bible Commentary*, Vol. 10. p. 501.

[7] It is possible that the sin is so egregious that some areas of service will be forever cut off from the forgiven saint regardless of the genuineness of his repentance. For example, a pastor who loses his blamelessness is likely to never return to a place of pastoral ministry. At the same time, there are no hard and fast rules about these things. It is up to each local church to determine what kind of Christian service the church members should perform.

[8] It has been my observation that such people are unwilling to listen to confrontation over their own sins. While they expect others to heed their counsel, even their commands at times, they quickly shut down any evaluation of their own sins.

if possible, between the smallest group, possibly between two individuals (v. 15). If resolution cannot be reached between the individuals involved in the conflict, others (mature believers) should be brought into the situation to help moderate a resolution (v. 16). Not only do these mature believers help provide perspective, they also help prevent a "he said-she said" situation where no one can tell who is being truthful. If that cannot resolve the conflict, then the offending party must be brought before the entire church. Believers who are led through church discipline to this point will generally seek repentance and restoration to the church (2 Cor. 2:6-10). If the individual will not repent, he demonstrates that he is not a true believer. The church should consider him to be unsaved and treat him accordingly (Matt. 18:17). He cannot remain a member of the church. Many Christians refuse to believe that it is their business to get this involved in the personal problems of other believers. They take the admonition to mind one's own business (see above) to the extreme of neglecting to demonstrate any concern for others. In reality, the church is the center of such adjudication (1 Cor. 6:5). Church leaders, particularly, should be willing to do the difficult work of confronting another leader, even a pastor, who is sinning against the Lord.[9]

Disunity can also be the result of doctrinal error. There are members who cause disunity in the church by spreading error, even false teaching. They cause divisions (*dichostasia*) in the church by arguing for an unbiblical position or elevating a minor doctrine to major status and censuring others who refuse to follow their lead. These are to be confronted with their error gently as the brother in Galatians 6:1. They should be identified (*skopeo*) as causing disunity and prevented from leadership in the church (*ekklino*). Their error encourages immature saints to follow their practices. Sometimes, such believers should be confronted publicly (Gal. 2:11). If their error damages the gospel or the testimony of the church, they should be called out for it. This should be done with great wisdom along with courage, not with a kind of bravado that desires to be known as the only one standing for the faith. That kind of spirit is the very one this entire teaching goes against.

---

[9] The process of such rebuke is found in 1 Timothy 5:19-20.

Finally, disunity can be the result of one or two who are ambitious to be "first" in the church (3 John 9). Like Diotrephes, they thrust themselves into leadership without the requisite qualifications. John writes about this man that "he loves to have preeminence (leadership authority) among them (the church) but will not receive us." Imagine what was going on in this church where even the apostle John was unwelcome. Leaders like this arrogantly assert their influence over others, bullying them into submission. The real church leaders should expose them before the congregation and refuse to follow them into folly. Such people will eventually leave the church and everyone will be better for it, even if such individuals are wealthy or influential. Peace is precious in the life of a church.

Moral sin. It is impossible to separate oneself from unbelievers who practice moral sin (1 Cor. 5:10). However, if someone professes to be a Christian and practices gross sin without repentance, he should be cut off from the church. Paul refers to this church discipline as giving the offending individual over to Satan (*paradidomi*) in order that his flesh should be destroyed (v. 5a). As harsh as this seems to be, especially to our modern way of thinking, this is actually the loving thing to do. The purpose of such an action is that "the spirit may be saved…" (v. 5b). People who profess to know Christ but are known to be living in gross sin should be confronted and expelled from the church unless they publicly repent of their sin. The kinds of sin the Scripture identifies as qualifying for this swift and complete judgment are sexual sins (*pornos*), covetousness, idolatry, abusive behavior, drunkenness or drug abuse, and stealing (v. 11). This list is probably not exhaustive. Any gross sin that is known throughout the church, or worse, in the community, must be confronted publicly in the hope that the offending individual will repent of that sin and be restored to fellowship with the church. If he refuses to repent, he indicates by his behavior that his profession of salvation is not genuine. He must be expelled from the church.

Moreover, there is no extended process by which repentance is gained. The process in Matthew 18 which refers to interpersonal conflict does not apply here. Paul writes that such individuals, when their sin is exposed, should be confronted at the next gathering of the church

(v. 4). In fact, Paul writes that he had already expelled the sinning individual in his heart (v. 3). These should be "put away" from among the congregation of saints (v. 13).

False teaching. The New Testament addresses the problem of false teachers in a number of instances. In particular, the two types of false teaching that manifested itself in the early church was Gnosticism and Judaizers. Gnostics were those who attempted to comingle Greek philosophy with Christianity and created a synthesized faith that purported to be greater than the basic teachings of the New Testament. Second century Christians were forced to confront this heresy head-on. Colossians and 1 John are notable in their defense of Christianity against the Gnostics. The Judaizers were the opponents of Paul who blended New Testament grace in Jesus with an adherence to Old Testament law. Paul addresses this problem in Galatians and Ephesians. Those who held to a circumcision saves position were teaching something that that Law itself never taught. Salvation is always by grace through faith in every dispensation.

Some false teachers were libertines who attempted to turn God's grace into a defense of sin, particularly gross sin. Both 2 Peter and Jude address this problem. These false teachers argued that they could sin without fear of consequences because of God's grace. Paul warned Timothy to be alert for such false teachers. They were encouraging insurrection against authorities (1 Tim. 6:2-3). The result of their teaching, according to Paul, was unnecessary conflict that harmed the gospel testimony of God's people. Instead of listening to the false teachers, believers should withdraw (*aphistemi*) from them.

General disobedience. This category is less defined than the previous two and the consequences are less severe. Paul writes the Thessalonians that disorderly believers (*ataktos*) should be admonished to do right. These are living "out of step" with how Christians should live. Instead of demonstrating a Christ-like behavior in actions and attitudes (1 Jn. 2:6), these reject the way of Christ taught in Scripture (2 Thess. 3:6). In the case of the Thessalonians, some of the believers were refusing to work and living off of the hard work of others within the congregation. Such idleness was disobedient to the teaching of Paul and the other apostles who commanded the people that any who will not work should not eat (v. 10). Even worse, such individuals were refusing to work to provide for themselves and were using their free time to stir up trouble in the church. This disobedient believers should be encouraged to repent of their behavior and adopt a lifestyle that is conducive to a positive Christian testimony (v. 12). If not, they should be shunned by the church but not like an unbeliever who is expelled from the congregation (vv. 14-15). Rather, the support he has been receiving from the church should be cut off and he should be publicly upbraided for his sinful behavior so that he experiences shame (*entrepo*).[10]

The Spirit of Accountability

There is a Christ-like gentleness that should be evident when confronting another believer over sin. There is no place for bitter partisanship among believers. That is not the wisdom of God on display (Ja. 3:13-14). Rather, such outbursts are evidence of an earthly,

animalistic, and demonic attitude (v. 15). God's wisdom is evident because it is true, is peaceful,

gentle, and reasonable. Such wisdom produces results that are not one-sided or false (v. 17).

Discipleship Questions

1. What is the basis of our Christian fellowship in a church?

---

[10] A final note is necessary to address how Christians should respond to professing believers who are not a part of the church (see chapter 2). Modern technology has created an environment where some are able to heavily influence church members even though they are not a part of that church. The use of the television, radio, and the internet allows some teachers great influence over wide sections of Christendom. *This is not spiritually healthy and not what God intended.* There are no super-apostles today. People who set themselves up as arbiters over larger groups of Christians do so outside the confines of Scripture. The New Testament never specifically address such individuals and never encourages this behavior. While some of these individuals are doctrinally sound, and some are incredibly helpful to Christians worldwide through their writing and speaking, they should be relegated to secondary status behind the local church pastor. He is God's shepherd for that congregation. Applications of separation outside the local church is not presented in Scripture and can only be inferred by applying these biblical principles to situations not directly addressed in the text.

2. In what ways do the three sins against fellowship—disunity, immorality, and general disobedience—threaten the church?

3. Is excommunication (church discipline) too harsh of a response for these sins?

4. How should a church approach someone who sins like this but also has a repentant spirit?

5. How should church members deal with a former member who has been put out of the church?

Chapter 12

Supporting the Church Financially

A long-time criticism of fundamentalist pastors is that they only preach on three topics; soul-winning, ecclesiastical and personal separation, and stewardship. Such criticism is not entirely unwarranted. Many ministries have been built off of heavy-handed pleas for money. Currently, popular radio talk show host Dave Ramsey encourages people to "live like no one else now" (pay off debt and save) so that you can "live and give like no one else tomorrow" (the benefits of wealth). His personal finances talk show is carried by 600+ radio stations and boasts upwards of 13 million weekly listeners.[1] His church-based program, Financial Peace University, is intended to help Christians learn money-management skills in order to help better themselves personally, and also learn to give to the church. The program is sold to pastors with *this* specific goal in mind.[2] His website promises that hosting his Financial Peace University will "create a culture of generosity" within the church.[3] Regardless whether his claim is true, the point is that stewardship is a considered to be a very important aspect of church life. Many well-known pastors have a yearly "stewardship" month and the giving texts of the New Testament including 1 Corinthians 16, 2

---

[1] Tim Alberta, "The Financial Whisperer to Trump's America," https://www.politico.com/magazine/story/2018/03/11/radio-dave-ramsey-2018-trump-217229, accessed May 15, 2019.

[2] A representative of Dave Ramsey's FPU called me personally and made a sales pitch for our church to use their program promising that it will grow the amount of money the church people give in the offerings. This was his specific selling point for the program.

[3] https://www.daveramsey.com/resources/church, May 15, 2019.

Corinthians 8-9, and Philippians 4 are utilized every year.

The Connection Between Giving and Worship

Earlier in this book, giving was presented as one of the elements of worship (chapter 4). Because worship is such an important part of the Christian life, and because giving is a part of that worship to God, giving is not an unimportant topic. This has been universally believed from the beginning of the church. There is no question that the early church gave offerings to the Lord (1 Cor. 16:1). How those offerings were taken, their frequency and purpose are all up for some debate. The early church leaders did not write very much about giving which should not be taken as its relative unimportance. One exception is Clement of Rome who refers to giving offerings in chapter 40 of his first epistle to the Corinthians. His real purpose in making the reference is to encourage orderliness in the Corinthian church.[4] Later, the Reformers addressed the subject in various ways either in a discussion of tithing or giving offerings. Church history is filled with references the importance of giving offerings as part of the believer's worship of God.

The Old Testament Tithe

Most considerations of Old Testament tithing begin prior to Moses and focus on the practices of Abel, Abraham, and Jacob.[5] By appealing to the time before the Law proponents of tithing argue that its early adoption automatically makes tithing a cross-dispensational mandate. Thus, some argue that every Christian is required to tithe (to give the tenth) similar to the way that Old Testament saints tithed and that Israel was commanded to tithe by God. This argument purports that

---

[4] See Clement of Rome, *The First Epistle of Clement to the Corinthians*, 40. http://www.newadvent.org/fathers/1010.htm, May 15, 2019.

[5] David A. Croteau, unpublished dissertation "A Biblical and Theological Analysis of Tithing: Toward a Theology of Giving in the New Covenant Era," p. 69.

Abel's sacrifice was accepted by God because it was a proper tithe (Gen. 4:3-7).[6] Likewise, both Abraham and Jacob give offerings of ten percent to God (Gen. 14:18-20, 28:13-22). It is unclear, however, that these offerings were anything close to the Jewish practice of tithing.

The Mosaic law covers the issue of tithing in Leviticus 27:30-33, Numbers 18:20-28, and Deuteronomy 14:22-29. The Numbers text is most interesting because it includes a tithe to the Levites, and then a subsequent tithe from the Levites to the priests. The result of Mosaic instruction on tithing is that Israel's expected contribution was greater than 10% of one's individual income. The expected annual contribution was about 20%.[7]

Post-exilic prophets also covered the subject of tithing. Most of the writing in these prophets deals with the importance of rebuilding Jerusalem after its destruction by the Babylonians (Neh. 10:37-39, 13:5, 12; Hag. 1:4-6, 2:6-9; Mal. 3:6-12). The Malachi text is one that has been abused by manipulative preachers and even those who are well-intentioned but totally misunderstand the prophet's message.[8] Malachi commands the people to bring their tithes into the storehouse. It is evident that this is not a reference to the church.[9] Tithing is an Old Testament command that was given by God to ancient Israel. It is not given as a rule that every Christian must follow. Moreover, it is clear that the tithe commands of the Mosaic Law have been fulfilled in the New Testament.[10]

---

[6] Ibid, 70-71.

[7] Ibid, 98.

[8] See Bobby Eklund and Terry Austin, *Partners with God: Bible Truths about Giving*, pp. 68-70. These writers claim that Christians who are struggling financially might be in a position of being cursed by God for their lack of tithing. "Anyone struggling financially should examine this area first." Even if this is a well-meaning statement, it is incredibly manipulative of believers, particularly immature saints. Who does not want to be blessed by God? To argue that a lack of financial blessing might be the result of failure to perform an Old Testament Israel task is the very definition of manipulation. It causes the immature to think, "if I do this, then God will do that." The motive is always more money or greater blessing.

[9] David A. Croteau, unpublished dissertation "A Biblical and Theological Analysis of Tithing: Toward a Theology of Giving in the New Covenant Era," p. 119.

[10] David A. Croteau, unpublished dissertation "A Biblical and Theological Analysis of Tithing: Toward a Theology of Giving in the New Covenant Era," p. 237.

The Tithing Principle in the New Testament

The fundamental question is: What value do these Old Testament passages on tithing have for the New Testament believer? First, it demonstrates the importance of obedience to God's commands. There are many commands in the Old Testament that have no direct relation to New Testament believers. That does not mean those commands are worthless or just "filler" information in the Old Testament. These commands were recorded and preserved for a variety of reasons; for our salvation and spiritual growth (2 Tim. 3:15-17), for our encouragement (Rom. 15:4), and for our warning (1 Cor. 10:11).[11] The Old Testament records examples of people who failed to obey God in various ways. Disobedience is always presented as a serious offense against God (1 Sam. 15:22-23).

Second, the direct command to tithe is nowhere repeated in the New Testament outside of the gospels and the principle of tithing is demonstrated in passages that address giving. The text that most directly draws from the Old Testament sacrifice command is Philippians 4:15-18. The Macedonian saints, concerned for Paul's welfare, had given him a gift even though they were quite poor themselves. This gift was greatly needed and Paul was thankful for their generous support (v. 16). He refers to their offering as having "an odor of sweet smell, a sacrifice acceptable, well-pleasing to God" (v. 18). This is a reference to the Old Testament Levitical sacrifices. While the Macedonians did not give out of a tithing requirement, their gift was entirely voluntary, Paul recognized it as similar as the Levitical offerings of the Old Testament.

Third, the tithing principle reminds us that giving offerings to the Lord is primarily about worship, not about how the money that is given is used. In ancient Israel, the people of God brought their best gifts to the Lord and gave them over to be sacrificed. From their hand to the altar, there was no purpose of that gift other than it was part of their devotion to God. After the sacrifice, some of it was used to help provide

---

[11] These are the biblically stated reasons for the recording of the Old Testament and its applicability to New Testament believers. Every sermon deals, at least in principle, with one of these three areas—salvation and spiritual growth, encouragement, or warning.

for the Levites and priests, and to provide for the costs of maintaining the tabernacle and later, the temple, but that was not the primary reason for the gift. Likewise, when a New Testament believer offers his gift in the offering it is not primarily for anything other than worship even if that money is later used to provide for the pastor, missionaries, the poor, and building projects and maintenance. "Many people seem to think that the reason we have an offering during the Sunday morning service is because the church needs to pay its bills and also wants to do good things with the money that is collected. Your church does need to pay its bills, and it probably does good things with the money …but that is *not* why we have an offering during the Sunday morning service."[12] The reason for an offering is because it is part of our worship to God. It is something that we own that we give up to God voluntarily.

The Use of Offerings

Even though New Testament offerings are voluntary gifts of worship to God, they are used in the local church to provide for its necessary function. There are four basic uses of offerings: to provide for the pastor, to support missionaries, to help the poor, and to provide for a church facility. Each of these is important to the healthy finances of a church.

Pastoral Compensation

There are organizations that set try to help churches determine how a pastor should be compensated and these generally rely on various things such as experience, longevity, education, and the size of the congregation. The Bible does not necessarily take any of these into account. 1 Corinthians 9 presents a biblical argument that pastors should be paid for their work (v. 11). Moreover, Paul encourages the church to consider paying a good pastor more money (1 Tim. 5:17-18). How much a pastor should make, however, is nowhere addressed in the New Testament. This is a local church matter. Each congregation determines for itself what it will pay the pastor(s).

---

[12] Mark Allan Powell, *Giving to God*, p. 11.

Missionaries

Missionaries usually need financial assistance. Paul connected the gift of the Macedonians to his gospel ministry (Phil. 1:5). Their financial help made them partners with him in his missions work. Many missionaries are underfunded because there are so few churches giving to missions as they should. These missionaries, evangelist-church planters (Eph. 4:11), are a gift of God to His church. They are the ones who establish new churches and their ministry is vital to the expansion of the gospel and obedience to the commission of Christ (Matt. 28:19-20). Every believer should purpose to give generously to missions as part of lifestyle. This should be something done primarily through his local church.

The Poor

Jesus stated that there will always be poor people (Jn. 12:8). This should not be taken as a statement to ignore poverty. Christians should not be discouraged from giving to the poor because poverty is a permanent feature of this world. Rather, Jesus' statement is one of opportunity. There will always be poor people who can use your help. Seen this way, giving to the poor is not a task to be taken as one of necessity, as a burden, but as a great blessing from God. It is the believer's privilege to help the poor. This was the determination of the first general church council held in Jerusalem. One of the things they encouraged the Gentile churches in Asia Minor to do was to provide for the poor (Gal. 2:10). Every church should consider its ministry to the poor in its community as an extension of the love of Jesus to others, not because they deserve it, but because of God's love and grace.

The Church Building

Church buildings are not present in the New Testament. The canon closed before church buildings became an issue. The early church were forced out of the synagogues, something Jesus warned His disciples would happen (Jn. 16:2). In Ephesus, Paul left the synagogue because of the hardness of the Jews to the gospel (Acts 19:9). The Ephesian church to the school of Tyrannus. Many of the early churches met in the homes of wealthier members (Phm. 2). As Christianity flourished, even in times of great persecution, church buildings were constructed. Many pastors today draw parallels between the Old Testament wall or temple passages such as in Haggai and Nehemiah to encourage giving to building projects or maintenance. The comparisons are not one-to-one, but the spirit of giving to the Lord's work is stressed as being important for God's people.

The Right Attitude

If a believer has a right view of Scripture, he will recognize that giving to the Lord is a blessing, a privilege. It is one of the things that believers should enjoy most about gathering together every week. Instead of feeling pressure to give a tithe, these believers happily give out of the abundance of what God has provided for them (1 Cor. 16:2). This generous and cheerful gift is part of their joyful worship to God.

This right spirit begins with Holy Spirit control. The Jerusalem church, persecuted for the testimony of Jesus, was so moved by the Spirit that many of them actually sold their possessions and gave it to the church (Acts 4:35). This is the first recorded New Testament offering. There was, apparently, no burden of obedience to any Old Testament tithe requirement, particularly in the Gentile church. Rather, the *heart* behind the gift was indicative of the Holy Spirit's control (v. 31).

Those who give themselves first to the Lord, are more willing to part with their temporary possessions as part of their worship to an eternal God (2 Cor. 8:5). The greater one's devotion to Christ and the more one is thankful for his salvation, the greater his gift to the Lord for God's blessing (Lk. 7:36-50). The more he sees his gift in light of God's greater gift of Christ (2 Cor. 8:9).

The right spirit includes a recognition that material things are temporary. The things that are visible (created things) are temporal (2 Cor.

4:18). Spiritual things are eternal. Those who lay up earthly treasures will be greatly disappointed when they are lost (Matt. 6:19). Those who lay up spiritual treasures will rejoice in eternity because such treasures can never be lost. They are everlasting.

The right spirit also includes the knowledge of how God's economy functions. There is a sowing and reaping principle in grace giving (2 Cor. 9:6). Those who give generously to God expect God's continued blessing. This should not be misconstrued to be that a financial offering will result in greater financial blessings as if giving offerings is some sort of material investment in God. That is not what the sowing and reaping principle teaches. Rather, those who give to God generously know that God will bless them, often in other ways, because no one can "out give" God. God loves someone who gives unprompted and with a willing heart (v. 7).

Finally, the right spirit always conceals what is given lest Satan use the gift as a temptation to pride. Jesus warned that people should give without the right hand and the left hand being in sync (Matt. 6:3).

Not About a Percentage

New Testament giving is not about giving "the tenth." It is about giving back to God a material offering freely and generously. New Testament giving is a recognition that everyone one has comes from God (Ja. 1:17). It is a thankful, worshipful response to God's blessing. It is also a recognition that God owns everything anyway. It is all His (Ps. 24:1). What monetary blessings we enjoy now are simply gifts from His hand to ours. He owns all the wealth of the earth (Hag. 2:8). Whether you give much or just a little, God watches over all. He sees what we give and internal motives for each gift (Mark 12:41-44). Instead of becoming a mindless automaton with your giving, simply functioning from a sense of duty, or worse, a sense of fear, give to God generously knowing that it brings Him pleasure. Give according to how He has prospered you (1 Cor. 16:2).

What if a Christian believes he cannot give because of severe financial crisis? It may be that his ability to give consistently may be limited by economic hardship. This is why attitude is more important than percentage. There are widows in the church who have only two pennies, but they are strong in faith and willing give what they have to the Lord. Being poor or on a strict budget because of debt does not mean one cannot give. Rather, it means poorer believers should be wise about how they give. A good pastor can provide guidance as to how to give in such situations. In doing this, even the poorest can enjoy the blessing of worshipping God through giving.

Discipleship Questions

1. Do you give regularly to your local church?

2. How should we think about supporting pastors and missionaries?

3. What is wrong with ministries that encourage people to give to them with a promise that God will richly reward them for their offering?

4. Do you think giving should be tied to a percentage (*not the position of this book*)? Why or why not?

Chapter 13

Community and Cultural Engagement

THE world's largest idol of the Hindu god Murugan is expected to be erected (2020) about 30 miles from Raleigh, North Carolina. The idol, and an accompanying temple, has not yet been built, but Hindu organizers are working diligently to obtain the necessary permits in order to begin construction. The size of the idol is incredible. It is actually four feet *taller* than the Statue of Liberty in New York.[1] What is most important, however, is that Murugan is a god of war. He holds a "divine spear" among other weapons which show his power to protect his followers.[2] The erection of this idol is not a contribution to culture and architecture in the Southeast. It is an assault on the authority and deity of Jesus Christ. It is a violation of the first and second commandments (Ex. 20:3-6). It is evidence of a rising demonic influence in America (1 Cor. 10:19-20). This proposed idol should trouble everyone who professes Christ (Acts 17:16). His presence is a contradiction of the gospel of Jesus. In the heart of the "Bible Belt," there may soon be one of the largest idols in the world.[3]

---

[1] Zachary Horner, "Hindu Temple Headed for Banks of Deep River," https://www.chathamnewsrecord.com/stories/hindu-temple-headed-for-banks-of-deep-river,1845?, accessed May 17, 2019.

[2] https://mythology.net/hindu/hindu-gods/murugan/, accessed May 17, 2019.

[3] Matt Rosenberg, "The Bible Belt in the United States," https://www.thoughtco.com/the-bible-belt-1434529, accessed May 17, 2019.

Local Application of the Great Commission

What solution do Christians have for idolatry? Should believers willingly give up hard-fought ground to Satan? Should public opposition from our adversary push us toward increasing isolation? There are some who believe isolation is the future of American Christianity. As Western Civilization becomes increasingly less Christian, some are considering "creative, communal solutions" as the only option if Christians are to "hold onto our faith and our values in a world growing ever more hostile to them."[4] This approach is known as "the Benedict Option," taking its name from a 6th century monk who chose to live in a forest, and later a cave outside of Rome. His monastic influence expanded as he developed twelve monasteries in the area.[5] While creating and joining monasteries is an unbiblical response to the present spiritual crisis, it may be that Christians are naturally banding together in other ways.[6]

The Argument for Isolationism

While most Christians are loathe to join a monastery, isolationism is not confined to a monastic lifestyle. Many have advocated for increased isolation from community and culture. Some in the Christian School Movement that began in the 1960's, and the Homeschool Movement that developed later see these options as opportunities to isolate themselves from a sinful culture. Other examples of Christian isolationism could be things like Christian business directories, social clubs, and charities. Individually, they may not be entirely isolationist, but they provide opportunity for some to almost entirely withdraw themselves from most contact with unbelievers.

The primary reason for Christian isolationism, at least in a relatively free society, involves a fear of close relationships with the world. The reason for this fear appears to be defensible.

---

[4] Rod Dreher, *The Benedict Option*, p. 2.
[5] Ibid. p. 14.
[6] The mega-church movement may be an inadvertent attempt to form large communities of Christians that have more political, economic, and societal influence than many small, independent churches. Some members of large churches boast that all of their social activities are only with other Christians. This may be a form of isolation.

- The world hates our Lord (Jn. 15:18).

- The world hates believers (1 Jn. 3:13).

- The world is a temptation for believers (2 Tim. 4:10).

- The world is a danger for believers (1 Jn. 2:15-17).

- The world is ruled by Satan (1 Jn. 5:19).

What rational Christian would want go out into a world like that? The temptation to withdraw from such a society appears, at least with these verses in mind, to be the more normative position for a follower of Jesus. If a believer reads this list you would expect him to say, "I don't want anything to do with the world."

One pastor, commenting on the drift towards worldliness in the Church, wrote his concern that Christians are in danger of losing all distinctiveness from the unsaved. "Today, the greatest challenge facing American evangelicals is not persecution from the world, but seduction by the world."[7] Another wrote a similar warning: "Today, it is not Big Brother who controls us but Big Pleasure. And the oppression that the pursuit of pleasure exerts is far more controlling than fear because pleasure rules from the inside."[8] Because the world is so dangerous, so deadly, *some* withdrawal *seems* to makes sense.

What Did Jesus Know?

The problem with isolationism is that it creates the possibility that the Church may fail to obey the last command of Jesus. This became apparent in the middle of the coronavirus pandemic. With Christians in quarantine and churches closed except for online services, there was a sort of isolationism that naturally occurred as a result. This was a

---

[7] C.J. Mahaney, *Worldliness*, p. 22.
[8] R. Kent Hughes, *Set Apart: Calling a Worldly Church to a Godly Life*, p. 20.

problem for many pastors because they knew the responsibility Christians have to share their faith. Each of the Gospels record some version of the Great Commission (Matt. 28:19-20, Mk. 16:15, Lk. 24:46-48, Jn. 20:21). Another version is repeated by Jesus prior to His ascension (Acts 1:8). A synthesis of these five texts indicate clearly that the mission of every disciple is to carry the gospel message to the world.

Matthew 28:19-20. The famous passage called the "Great Commission" begins with the imperative command "go."[9] The followers of Jesus were to go into the world with the gospel. It has been understood by many throughout Church History that this command was not just for the disciples of Jesus' own day, but for all of His followers throughout this dispensation. Christians today have the obligation to take the gospel into the world.

A Natural Tension. This creates a tension between a rational fear of the world and an obedient response to what Jesus commanded. Believers of every era have wrestled with how to fulfill the Lord's command and not be swept away by the ugly tide of worldliness. As the message of Jesus spread through Jerusalem, particularly after Peter healed the lame man (Acts 3), problems with how Christians should interact with unbelievers arose. When persecution forced Christians out of Jerusalem, they took with them the gospel of Jesus and the Church grew to more than just an seeming offshoot of Judaism. Paul's missionary ministry took the gospel through the Roman Empire. The statement of Jesus (Acts 1:8) came to pass as the gospel spread from Jerusalem and Judea to Samaria (Acts 8), and then to the uttermost parts of the earth. It is still spreading today around the world.[10]

What Cannot Be. Obedience to this command, as important as it is, cannot mean an acceptance of worldliness. By the time John wrote his first epistle warning against worldliness, the Church had spread throughout the entire Middle East and into Europe. Tradition

---

[9] See Daniel B. Wallace's footnote in *Greek Grammar: Beyond the Basics,* p. 642. Wallace explains that the participle "go" should not be translated as "having gone" or "as you are going." The best translation is to read "go!"

[10] See F. F. Bruce, "The Book of Acts," *The New International Commentary on the New Testament,* p. 39.

teaches that some of the disciples took the gospel into Africa and others into India. There is some question as to whether Paul eventually traveled to Spain, but archeological discoveries have revealed that the gospel spread north as far as the United Kingdom. John probably wrote his epistle from Ephesus.[11] The gospel did not remain contained in Jerusalem. They were witnesses for Jesus to the uttermost parts of the earth. The consequence of this is that John's warning against worldliness is not justification for isolationism. Jesus would never have ordered His disciples into a situation that would have caused them to sin. Fear of worldliness is no excuse for disobedience to Jesus' command to "go."

Two Insane Approaches

Modern evangelicalism struggles with this tension. Christians want to be in the world (evangelism), but avoid being influenced negatively by the world (worldliness). This struggle has resulted in a few extreme responses to the natural tension of being "in" the world but not "of" it. These extreme responses can be labeled contextualization and anticulturalization.

Contextualization. One extreme response is to determine the validity of one's approach to the world by its outcome. This kind of pragmatism argues that the divine emphasis on evangelism justifies adopting some worldly means. Evangelical scholars refer to this as "contextualization" and they cite 1 Corinthians 9:22 and Acts 17:23 as support for their argument. "Contextualization is the idea that we need to be translating gospel truth into language understood by our culture. [Christians] have been doing this for centuries. They take the unchanging truth of the Gospel and put it into language that fits the context they are trying to reach."[12] There are a couple of problems with this argument. First, neither 1 Corinthians 9:22 or Acts 17:23 support an adoption of worldly

---

[11] D. A. Carson and Douglas Moo, *An Introduction to the New Testament*, KL 16517.

[12] See Rob Wilkerson's quotation of Tullian Tchividjian from his book *Unfashionable.* http://www.robwilkerson.net/2010/05/contextualization-without-compromise-by.html, accessed May 20, 2019.

practices in order to reach unbelievers. For example, being "all things to all men" (1 Cor. 9:22) does not mean Paul took on the mantle of worldliness in order the reach people for Christ. In a modern context, Paul would not have frequented bars swilling beers and joining in drunken frivolity in order to share the gospel.[13] Rather than unleashing his Christian liberty, the point of 1 Corinthians 8-10 is to demonstrates ways Paul restricted his liberty so as to not harm the gospel. His argument (9:22) must be understood within the overall context. Paul explains in chapter 9 that he deserved financial compensation from the Corinthians, but that he restricted this liberty because he did not want to harm the gospel (v. 15). Instead of delimiting himself, Paul restricted himself. Instead of exercising his freedom from all men, he made himself a servant of all (v. 19). Thus, to the Jews, he became a Jew (v. 20). To the Gentiles, he became a Gentile. This is not contextualization in the sense that Paul adopted Jewish or Gentile worldliness. Paul limited his behavior in order that his Christian liberty did not offend others. This is really the exact opposite of how many evangelicals think of contextualization. Moreover, his willingness to quote secular Greek poets is not an example of this kind of contextualization either (Acts 17:28). Paul's approach to the Athenians is an example of him explaining that the gospel makes rational sense to a group of philosophers. It is not an example of Paul becoming secular in order to reach secular people.[14]

Anticulturalization. If the first extreme is an adoption of nearly everything in the world in order to win the world, the second extreme is the opposite; a rejection of culture entirely. In an almost Amish-like manner, these Christians reject modern culture. They adopt codes of conduct, particularly for dress and hair styles that are purposefully 20-30 years behind modern culture. They do this because they connect culture (defined: "how people live") with worldliness. If this was math, the problem would look like this: culture = worldliness.

---

[13] Jonathan Serrie, "Beer Evangelists Spread the Gospel at Bars," https://www.foxnews.com/food-drink/beer-evangelists-spread-the-gospel-at-bars, accessed May 20, 2019.

[14] See Phil Johnson, "Paul on Mars Hill," http://www.thegracelifepulpit.com/Sermons.aspx?code=2007-11-03b-PJ, accessed May 20, 2019.

The problem with this argument is that it is not culture that is worldly, but worldly culture that is worldly. When John warns the believers in Ephesus to reject the world, he specifies that worldliness is a love for the things in the world that specifically appeal to one's own earthly lusts such as the flesh, the eyes, and the pride of life (1 Jn. 2:16). This is similar to the Lord's command to refrain from storing up earthly treasures (Matt. 6:19). It really does not matter if one is laying up treasures on earth while dressed in styles 30 years behind the modern day. It is still worldliness. A total rejection of modern culture (think: Amish) makes one appear to the world as strange and out of touch with reality, not as more godly or pious. This approach was not the one taken by the apostles of Jesus. While they rejected the world, they operated within their culture.

Examples of Community and Cultural Engagement in Acts

Both approaches (contextualization and anticulturalization) are extreme responses to the problem of reaching out to the world with the gospel without being swallowed up by it. A study of Acts demonstrates that the early ministries of the apostles did not fall into either extreme. As referred to above, Acts can be divided into three major sections according to Acts 1:8. The ministry in Jerusalem is in Acts 1-7. The ministry in Judea and Samaria is in Acts 8-11:18. The ministry to the uttermost is in Acts 11:19-28:31.[15] These ministries are prime examples of community and cultural engagement of the church to unbelievers. In fact, as the theme of Acts is "witness," this study is very helpful in determining the means and methods used in the first century and how those might be utilized today.[16]

My interpretation of the Acts account is as follows.

---

[15] F. F. Bruce, "The Book of Acts," *The New International Commentary on the New Testament*, p. 39.

[16] See the footnotes on Acts 1:8 by Stewart Custer, *Witness to Christ*, pp. 4-6. He provides a very helpful resource on the words "witness" and "testimony."

Acts 1–7. The early portion of Acts reveals the rapid expansion of Christianity in Jerusalem after the ascension of Jesus (1:9). The institution of the church coincided with Pentecost, a festival held in Jerusalem commemorating God giving Moses the Law at Sinai.[17] As one of Judaism's annual pilgrimages, the population in Jerusalem would have been quite large. It is no coincidence that the Holy Spirit came at the festival when the Jews celebrating the coming of the Law.[18] One dispensation was giving way to another. Peter's sermon at Pentecost was to a large group of Jews and proselytes who were in Jerusalem for the festival (Acts 2:9-10). Luke records that 3,000 of them came to faith in Jesus at the conclusion of the sermon (v. 41). Chapter 2 ends with the Jerusalem church thriving as God was daily adding to their number (v. 47). The situation in chapter 3, Peter's healing of the lame man in the name of Jesus, thrust the Jerusalem church into the forefront of Jewish life. The story is illustrative of how God was increasing the influence of the church.[19] The healing of the lame man completely changed the way the early Christians were received by the people. The situation became so dire for the Jewish religious leaders, that they imprisoned some of the disciples. This did not discourage their influence. The church continued to grow (4:4). Satan's frontal assault on the church was unsuccessful. His next attempt was to destroy the church from within. The early church faced three important challenges of which Satan was the obvious source of at least one (5:3). He tempted Ananias and Sapphira to sin in hopes of gaining leadership in the church.[20] Except for Peter's direct intervention, this might have destroyed the Jerusalem church. Instead, the deaths of this couple caused the people to fear God more (v. 11). The second challenge, the problem of the Grecian widows (6:1), may not have been from Satan, but it was just as serious. The church was in danger of splitting apart along cultural lines. The institution of deacons helped solve the problem as these devoted themselves to serving the physical needs of the people (6:2). The result

---

[17] Richard Longnecker, "Acts," *The Expositor's Bible Commentary*, Vol. 9, p. 269.
[18] Ibid.
[19] Ibid, p. 292.
[20] Compare what this couple did (5:1-2) with what Barnabas did (4:37).

was an increased in the number of believers including those who had been in the Jewish priesthood (6:7). The third challenge was the arrest and trial of Stephen, one of the early deacons in Jerusalem (6:9-12). His defense of the gospel to the Sanhedrin ends this section with his martyrdom (7:60). Think about all of the ways in which the Jerusalem church was involved in its community: Pentecost, the healing of the lame man at the temple, the deacon ministry to the needy. All of these show involvement, not isolation, in the community in Jerusalem.

Acts 8:1-11:18. Stephen's death broke through the barrier of the Jews tolerating the Christians in Jerusalem. It opened new avenues of persecution against believers. God scattered the church as a result of this aggression (8:1). The focus shifts away from Jerusalem to Judea and Samaria (8:1, 5). This only increased with the conversion of Saul (Paul) (9:6). This section contains Peter's ministry to Cornelius, a Roman centurion (10:1).

Acts 11:18-28:31. After a brief mention of Peter's rescue by the angel (12:7-11), the remainder of Acts follows Luke's diary of Paul's three missionary journeys ending with his first imprisonment in Rome. Each missionary journey is notable for the way Paul uses every opportunity to share the gospel with unbelievers. Luke includes:

- His interaction with a politician (13:8)

- His influence in a city that included almost the entire town (13:44)

- Works of mercy among the sick (14:10)

- His joining in religious services (16:13)

- His interaction with a jailer (16:27-31)

- The church plant in Thessalonica (17:1-2)

- His evangelistic sermon on Mars Hill (17:23)

- His occupation and the people involved in it (18:2-3)

- His use of the school of Tyrannus (19:9)

- His influence in a local economy (19:27)

- His interaction with the Romans (21:37)

- His appeal to Caesar based on his citizenship (25:11)

- His interaction with a king (26:27)

- His encouragement of the sailors (27:10-11)

- His influence on Melita when gathering sticks for a fire (28:6)

- His discussion with the Jews in Rome (28:17)

Everywhere Paul went he used the situation he was in as a spring-board for the gospel. These were not formal events primarily. They were just part of the way in which he engaged people in his community and culture. This is what the church should also be doing. Believers should use their own life circumstances as opportunities to engage people with the gospel. Thus, Christians can live and work "in" the world without being "of" the world. Believers should be a gospel light in a spiritually dark place. The goal should not be to adopt worldly means in order to "help" the light be more effective. God's light does not need help. It dispels darkness really well on its own. It just needs to shine.

Discipleship Questions

1. What spiritual force is behind idolatry?

2. What is wrong with the "Benedict Option?"

3. How should Christians approach their culture?

4. How influential was Paul's ministry on the culture different cities in the Roman Empire?

5. What can we do spread the gospel better?

Chapter 14

World Evangelism

THE change is so different it is almost impossible to miss. Jesus sent out His disciples to "the house of Israel" (Matt. 10:6). He limited their ministry to only the Jews. They were not to evangelize the Gentiles or even the Samaritans. This limitation sounds strange to the modern Christian's ear, especially if one has grown accustomed to missionary sermons on the Great Commission. How is it that Jesus commissioned His disciples to purposefully avoid non-Jews? Yet, there it is in print: "do not go into the way of the Gentiles... (v. 5). This was before Jesus died on the cross. After His death and resurrection, He commissioned these same disciples to go to the nations (*ethnos*). What ethnic limitations were previously in place were now lifted. Jesus' intent was that the gospel should be spread throughout the whole world (Mk. 16:15).

The great evangelistic efforts were to originate in Jerusalem (Lk. 24:27). The disciples were commissioned to take the gospel from Jerusalem into the surrounding districts (Acts 1:8).[1] They were not to

---

[1] Sometimes pastors refer to Jerusalem to mean the immediate area around the church. Like rings on a target, they label each expanding area. Judea and Samaria usually mean regions. The uttermost means other countries. This is, most likely, not a good interpretation of the verse. Jesus is not giving every Christian a plan for world evangelism ("start in your 'Jerusalem' and work outward") but actually the plan for His disciples at that time. They were to remain in Jerusalem until they received the Spirit (Acts 1:4). Afterward, they were to take the gospel outward with Jerusalem as the epicenter of Christianity. This also explains what Paul means in Romans 1:16. The gospel began with the Jews and then was taken to the Gentiles. This does not mean that evangelism should always begin with the Jews as some suppose. It is just a statement of fact. The gospel began in Jerusalem and then moved outward through Judea and Samaria finally reaching the uttermost, the Gentiles.

stop until the uttermost (*eschatos*) was reached with the truth that Jesus saves. They were to share with everyone the good news that Jesus died for sin, was buried, but rose from the dead (1 Cor. 15:3-4). How far away is the uttermost? The word sometimes means last or final referring to a place in time. The *eschaton* is the root word for eschatology, the study of last things or the end times. It can also mean something extreme. In this case, the context indicates that the extremity is a location. The uttermost is the farthest point away from Jerusalem. The Great Commission is a mandate to missions. It is a direct order from the commanding officer to the soldiers of the realm to take the message of the gospel to every corner of the earth.

Those in Darkness

Many theologians believe that the Apostle John wrote the Gospel of John around 85 A.D. It was a period of time that must have seemed particularly dark. Jerusalem was in shambles, destroyed by the Romans about fifteen years earlier. The early disciples of Jesus obeyed His command to spread the gospel and it had overflowed the confines of Jerusalem and Judea so that Christianity was spread throughout the Roman Empire. Yet, powerful new forces threatened to destroy the gospel. Christians were under persecution in various localities throughout the Empire. Judaism was making inroads in bringing weak Christians back to law-keeping. Gnosticism was blossoming as a philosophy and threatened to undermine the faith that Jesus is all one needs for salvation. Greek and other pagan philosophies were mixing with some Christian concepts and forming a syncretistic religion (see Colossians). The world was spiritually dark.

There were already three Gospels circulating among the churches and they were very helpful in solidifying the faith of believers in Jesus. Matthew was very effective in reaching Jews for Christ. Mark and Luke were effective in reaching Gentiles. Even so, the story of Jesus was not quite complete. God had one more Gospel record to be written and the Spirit used John to write it.

How John's Gospel begins is of great significance. The first sentence makes clear that there was a Word (*logos*) which was God (1:1). He was with (*pros*) God and in the beginning (*arche*) with God (v. 2). Moreover, the Word created all things (v. 3). He was the originator of all life (v. 4). John makes use of the words life and light almost interchangeably. Those who have light have life. Those who have life are in the light. More importantly, this Word became flesh, an obvious reference to Jesus (v. 14). Into the darkness of sinful mankind, Jesus brought the spiritual light of eternal life. He said as much plainly. Those who believe in Jesus, who follow Him will not order his life in darkness/death but have light/life (8:12).

This fact is highlighted throughout John's Gospel, particularly in chapters 3-9. Nicodemus represents the religiously blind who are trapped by their own self-righteousness (3:10). The Samaritan woman represents the morally blind trapped in a cycle of sinful behavior or addiction (4:29) very much like the woman who Jesus freed after being taken in the act of adultery (8:11). The lame man represents the spiritually helpless who are trapped in false hope (5:7). The crowd of thousands who were fed by Jesus, but ultimately left him represent those who seek the truth, but do not actually desire Christ (6:26, 41, 66). The disciples who remained represent those who trust in Jesus because they recognize God's revelation in Him (6:67-69). This truth climaxes in the healing of the blind man who becomes an illustration of how Jesus brings spiritual light to those in the darkness of sin (9:11).

The World Remains in Darkness

One of the ways the Bible describes unbelievers is that they are spiritually blind. This is the way Paul describes unsaved people to the Ephesians. Unbelievers order their lives according to their spiritually empty thoughts (Eph. 4:17). Their minds have been blinded by sin and the god of sin (Satan: 2 Cor. 4:4). They do not possess spiritual life. They have blind hearts (Eph. 4:18).

The result of this spiritual blindness and emptiness is evident in the life of sin that unbelievers forge for themselves. They believe the lie that they are open-minded, enlightened people even while God calls them fools (Rom. 1:22). They belittle God either through their idolatry (Eastern Civilization) or apathy (Western Civilization). The result is that they willingly accept dishonorable acts as normal and even acceptable (v. 24). They twist God's truth setting themselves up as the final authority (v. 25). They even attempt to normalize unnatural behavior (v. 27). Ultimately, they dive into the deep end of the depravity pool enjoying the gross sins of the flesh knowing that God hates it and will judge it, but they do not care (v. 32).

Taking God's Light to the World

The solution for the world's spiritual darkness is the light of the gospel. In God's infinite wisdom, He tasked believers with this responsibility. We who know God's light should be shining it into the darkness of the world. The Great Commission demands that those who have the gospel must share it with those who do not (Lk. 24:47). Our gospel is a light that radiates outward from our hearts even as it is progressively changing us to be more like Jesus (2 Cor. 3:18). It is not like the fading glory of the Law that gradually disappeared from Moses' face (v. 13). Paul's point is that as believers mature in Christ, they become an increasingly more effective witness for Christ. The more one is like Jesus, the greater his light shines into the dark world of sinners. The result is that the only people who cannot see the light are those who have been blinded by Satan (4:3). He does not want "the light of the glorious gospel of Christ" to "shine unto them" (v. 4).

What is really remarkable is that God has chosen us as vessels of this great gospel treasure. We are just clay pots; temporary, throw-away bags (v. 7). We are fragile beings susceptible to every kind of problem. We can be afflicted (*thlibo*), be set at loss with no earthly hope (*aporeo*), be mistreated (*dioko*), and thrown to the ground (*kataballo*) (vv. 8-9). Humanly speaking, there is not much to us. It would seem that we are the worst choice for who should care for this charge to share the gospel. Yet even as we are so seemingly frail, we carry about gospel truth that "the life of Jesus" is evident in us (v. 10). Compared to the glory of the gospel, we are just "jars of clay."[2]

Means for World Evangelism

With this great task of taking the gospel to the nations set before us, it is important to understand the means by which we must accomplish our mission. The first step is recognizing those who God has specially burdened for this task. Today, we refer to these people as missionaries. Paul called them evangelists (*euangelistes*), those who carry the good news of the gospel (Eph. 4:11). They are not evangelists in the sense of one who is an itinerant preacher, but rather "missionaries who pioneer outreach in areas where the faith has not as yet been proclaimed."[3] It is interesting to note that Timothy was commanded to "do the work of an evangelist" (2 Tim. 4:5). Every believer should be actively engaged in reaching his local community for Christ. The special ministry of evangelist, however, is for those who preach the gospel in order to plant churches.[4] Church planting is the essence of evangelism. It is the ultimate fulfillment of the Great Commission. "This must be the heart of every pastor and every church, for every church has been given the responsibility—to evangelize the world by starting churches."[5]

Recognition of missionaries is one of the important jobs of the local church. Like the great Gentile church in Antioch who commissioned Paul and Barnabas for their first missionary journey (Acts 13:2), local churches today recognize and commission missionaries to carry the gospel to the "uttermost." This is accomplished through prayer, an emphasis on church planting, and providing opportunities for young men to train for vocational ministry. Church planters should be qualified for pastoral ministry like pastors (see chapter 6).

---

[2] Murray J.Harris, "2 Corinthians," *The Expositor's Bible Commentary*, Vol. 10, (Grand Rapids: Zondervan, 1976), p. 342.

[3] A Skevington Wood, "Ephesians," *The Expositor's Bible Commentary*, Vol. 11, (Grand Rapids: Zondervan, 1976), p. 58.

[4] Peter O'Brien, "The Letter to the Ephesians," *The Pillar New Testament Commentary*, (Grand Rapids: Eerdmans, 1999), p. 299.

[5] Bud Calvert, *God's Passion*, (Lancaster, CA: Striving Together Publications, 2010), p. 24.

Church Support

After a missionary is recognized[6] as being led by God to establish a new church, the local church must provide him with support. There are very few who are capable of doing the work of church planting on their own, and no one should attempt church planting without being commissioned by another church. Someone who starts churches without a sending church does so on his own authority, a very dangerous proposition.

Financial support. One of the things that encouraged the apostle Paul was how the Macedonian believers supported him financially, even though they were very poor themselves (2 Cor. 8:2). Paul was in prison because of his missionary work. When he wrote that he was the prisoner of Jesus, he meant that literally (2 Tim. 1:8). In all likelihood this meant that he was chained to Roman soldiers with iron shackles (Phil. 1:13). The Macedonian believers recognized that Paul needed help and sent a gift to meet his material needs (Phil. 4:14). He was so encouraged by their gift that even from prison he wrote "I have all, and abound: I am full... (v. 18). Their financial support came at just the right time. Consequently, because of their gift, Paul told them that he saw them as partners in his ministry (1:5).

Prayer support. After admonishing the believers in Ephesus to take God's own armor to themselves (Eph. 6:11), Paul encouraged them to pray for him specifically. This missions prayer was for boldness (parresia). Even Paul felt the need for encouragement to speak out for Jesus and the gospel (vv. 19-20). He gives similar reasons to the Colossian church (Col. 4:3-4). Paul recognized the importance of prayer in regards to missions. No missionary work is successful without prayer. When a church commissions a church planter or takes up the obligation to regularly support a missionary financially, there is accompanying duty to pray.

Relationships. Missions work is lonely and isolating. Like a laborer working at the farthest boundary of a farm, he may be part of the overall

---

[6] See Appendix 3 on ordination.

farming operation, but it *feels* like he works alone. Missionaries often live in a radically different culture from their own. They are separated by many miles from family and friends. Often this separation is not for a short time but for long stretches of time. Missions work can feel like serving a prison term even when the missionary is free to serve Christ in another country. One of the most important ministries a church has with a missionary is relational. Missionaries need other Christians to come alongside them and provide them needed emotional support as they work in relative isolation.

Visits. Finally, missionaries should not feel burdened to continually be contacting churches back home. The local church should take it as a ministry to visit the missionaries in their home. More than many other things, a visit from a pastor or a church member can bring great encouragement to continue serving Christ in a foreign culture. Paul told the Colossians that his interaction with Epaphras was encouraging to him (Col. 1:7-8). Visiting a missionary may seem expensive or like a vacation, but the value of the visit is incredible to God's servants who are stationed on the front lines in the spiritual war.

Challenges

It is unfortunate that many churches do not intentionally plant new churches. It should be something every church is doing intentionally. "Church planting is not optional."[7] A running joke among pastors is that a church split how some accomplish church planting. The new church, by the way, is often given a name like "New Hope Church" or "Harmony Baptist Church." It signifies the way the people feel in starting a new church as the result of conflict. Maybe the new church (as a result of a church split) should really be named honestly: "I'm Glad I No Longer Go There Bible Church." Church splitting is not church planting. The truth is that church planting is difficult, and there are many challenges preventing churches from planting new churches.

---

[7] Ibid, 25.

Geo-Political Considerations. In countries where there is some freedom of speech and churches are able to evangelize with relatively little fear of persecution, church planting is rare, but not impossible. Some countries have laws which make church planting a crime. North Korea is notorious for imprisoning and even murdering Christians for their faith. Countries like North Korea challenge Christians to come up with inventive and courageous ways to witness and plant churches.

Racism. In the centuries prior to the modern missions movement, the attitude existed which said if God wants to save the heathen, He can do it.[8] From the earliest days of the church, racism has discouraged missions. Paul wrote the Ephesians to encourage them that they were no longer strangers and foreigners to the family of God but were now fellow-citizens and saints standing on the foundation of the apostles and prophets, Jesus Christ Himself being the cornerstone (Eph. 2:19-20). When missionary John Paton announced that he was going to New Hebrides as a missionary, an older man in the church cautioned him against throwing his life away. "The Cannibals! You will be eaten by Cannibals!" This frustrated Paton to the point where the finally replied to the gentleman somewhat comically: "You are advanced in years now, and you own prospect is soon to be laid in the grave, there to be eaten by worms; I confess to you, that if I can but live and die serving and honoring the Lord Jesus, it will make no difference to me whether I am eaten by Cannibals or worms...."[9]

Church Growth. The mindset among evangelicals today is that a larger church is always better than a smaller one. The Church Growth Movement, something that began in the mid-Twentieth century, has almost entirely infected American evangelicalism. It began at Fuller Seminary in 1965 with a class on church growth taught by veteran missionary Donald McGavran.[10] Within 30 years, many evangelical

---

[8] A phrase similar to this is attributed to John Ryland speaking to a young William Carey. See Dan Graves, "Conversion of John Ryland, Carey's Friend," https://www.christianity.com/church/church-history/timeline/1701-1800/conversion-of-john-ryland-careys-friend-11630272.html, accessed May 22, 2019.

[9] James Paton, *John G. Paton: Missionary to the New Hebrides*, (Carlisle, PA: Banner of Truth Trust, 2002), p. 56.

[10] Howard Culbertson, "Donald McGavran and the Church Growth Movement," http://home.snu.edu/\textasciitilde{}hculbert/mcgavran.pdf, accessed May 22, 2019.

churches were refocusing their efforts on becoming larger, not repro-ducing more churches. This mindset is evident, even among those who claim to be disinterested.[11]

Few Missionaries. One of the biggest challenges to missions is the lack of Christians interested in the job. Most believers are content to live in the relative ease of a wealthy, industrialized society rather than relocating to a Third World country. While not everyone is burdened for missions, it is important that some young adults take on the re-sponsibility of church planting. Research into the age of pastors and missionaries reveals that only 33% are under 40 years old. 24% are over 56 years old. This is a big shift from the 1960s when more than half of pastors and missionaries were under 45 years old.[12]

One reason for this may be the problem of prolonged adolescence. This is not just a missions problem. This is an entire church leadership problem. Researchers are discovering that children are not maturing as quickly as in previous generations.[13] Some point to the smartphone as a cause of prolonged adolescence. "Today's teens follow a slow life strategy ... our current culture in the United States ...."[14] Whatever the cause, many young men are not capable of determining that God wants them in vocational ministry. The number of men training in Bible colleges and Seminaries is shrinking and this trend is not likely to change in the near future.

---

[11] See Gary L. McIntosh's book *One Size Doesn't Fit All* (Grand Rapids: Fleming Revell, 1999) for a good example of how some claim to be neutral on church size. The entire emphasis in the book, regardless of protests to the opposite, is on how larger churches are better than smaller churches.

[12] See George Barna, "The Aging of America's Pastors," https://www.barna.com/research/aging-americas-pastors/, accessed May 22, 2019.

[13] Brett Stetka, "Extended Adolescence: When 25 is the New 18," https://www.scientificamerican.com/article/extended-adolescence-when-25-is-the-new-18/?redirect=1, accessed May 22, 2019.

[14] Jean Twenge, *iGen: Why Today's Super-Connected Kids Are Growing Up Less Rebellious, More Tolerant, Less Happy—and Completely Unprepared for Adulthood,* (New York: Atria Books, 2018), KL 405.

Under Our Haystack

In August 1806, a group of five young men from Williamstown, Massachusetts gathered in a field to pray for foreign missions. A thunderstorm caused them to find refuge under a haystack. Their weekly prayer meetings forged into their minds the commitment to reach Asia with the gospel. Their motto was "We can do this, if we will." The results of this prayer meeting was enormous including the founding of the American Board of Commissioners for Foreign Missions. Today, there is a monument at the place where the five met for prayer. The monument reads "The Field is the World."[15]

Baptists need to adopt that same spirit today. It is long since past the need for another missions movement to take the gospel to the uttermost. If this is to be accomplished, three important things are necessary. First, Christians need to keep the goal in mind and not settle for current conditions. Jesus said that the goal is the whole world. While that seems impossible, there is no soul unfit for salvation by the atoning work of Jesus. Second, Christians must see themselves as "missionaries" at home in their own communities. With immigration increasing, American evangelicals have an opportunity to reach people from other cultures like never before. Third, churches need to resolve to plant more churches, not grow larger. Church growth is so attractive because it provides the impression of progress. New buildings are built. New friendships are forged. But if the growing church is only at the expense of older, smaller churches (Christians moving from smaller to larger churches), then no real advance is being made. Church planting is not easy. It takes financial commitment. I requires the church plant to go through deprivation and hardship. It takes a toll on the pastor and his family. Still, it is the best means for obeying the command of Jesus to take the gospel to the nations.

---

[15] Ronny Floyd, "When Was Your Church's Last Haystack Prayer Meeting?" https://www.christianitytoday.com/edstetzer/2019/march/when-was-your-churchs-last-haystack-prayer-meeting.html, accessed May 22, 2019.

Discipleship Questions

1. Whose responsibility is it to present the gospel to the unsaved world?

2. How can churches and Christians support missionaries better?

3. Which of the challenges to world evangelism do you think is the most difficult to overcome?

4. What would it take to begin a new missions movement?

Chapter 15

To God Be Glory in the Church

Tʜᴇʀᴇ are places in the Bible that stop the reader for a moment and require serious contemplation. Paul's prayer in Ephesians 3 is one of those places. Paul prays that the Ephesians would be given spiritual strength according to the riches of God's own glory (Eph. 3:16). This wealth of power is what accompanies the indwelling Christ, who permanently indwells every believer by the Holy Spirit (v. 17). The result is that the Christian is able to fully understand the incredible nature of Christ's love, something that is not naturally knowable (vv. 18-19). Many theologians have written lengthy explanations of this text and pastors have preached series of sermons on it. It is one of those important stopping places in Scripture. It is difficult to conceive of a prayer to God greater than this one.[1]

Doxology

The prayer ends with a doxology. It is directed towards God the Father. "Now unto Him ..." (v. 20). It reads literally "to him who is power" (*to de dunameno*). "The doxology begins with an ascription of power to God."[2] Everything that is accomplished in the individual believer's life and in the church is the result of obedience to the power of God.

---

[1] Francis Foulkes, "Ephesians," *The Tyndale New Testament Commentaries*, (Grand Rapids: Eerdmans, 1989), p. 114.

[2] Peter O'Brien, *The Letter to the Ephesians*, (Grand Rapids: Eerdmans, 1999), p. 267.

The apostles received power (dunamis) after the Holy Spirit indwelled them (Acts 1:8). There is no power, no ability to do anything of value that is not the direct result of God's own power.

His power, moreover, exceeds our expectation. The phrase "exceeding abundantly" means that there is no limit to what God can do. God's power supersedes all things. He is above all and over all. There is nothing more powerful than He.[3] We limit God's power because our minds are incapable of thinking about it to the degree to which it exists. We are limited by our own finiteness in conceptualizing it. As ancient man would not be able to understand modern technology without some frame of reference, so we are incapable of grasping the full nature of God's abundant power. It is just too high for us to know. The result is that we cannot ask or think in accordance to its greatness. "There is no limit what God can do."[4] The only thing limited is our ability to explain it.[5] It is outside our reality. This is why Christians need the Holy Spirit to help us pray. There is no possible way a believer can every fully understand how to pray as he ought to pray (Rom. 8:26). The fact that Paul at least knew that he could not fully comprehend God's power is evidence that he was much closer to the truth than most. Those who claim God's power as if they are some spiritual version of a comic superhero do not really understand what they are doing. They act as if speaking some magic words will give them "the power." This is complete nonsense. No one can comprehend God's power. There is nothing about God that a human being can fully understand. We cannot even come very close. The depths of the riches of God's wisdom and knowledge are unknowable (Rom. 11:33). God's power is incomprehensible.

God's Power at Work

At the same time, this power moves the church forward. It is that which causes the church to function operationally. Anything the

---

[3] Ibid.

[4] Ibid.

[5] Francis Foulkes, "Ephesians," *The Tyndale New Testament Commentaries*, (Grand Rapids: Eerdmans, 1989), p. 114.

church does that is good or valuable is the direct result of God's incomprehensible power working through it in order to accomplish God's own design.

There is some evidence that effectiveness of God's indwelling power is relative to the proportion of faith in each case. Some believers are seemingly more gifted than others and some churches appear to possess greater power of God than others. This is not because God's power is limited inherently, but because of some external reason that power is not as evident as it should be. For example, the unbelief in Jesus' hometown regarding His person and ministry limited the works that Jesus could do there. It was not that Jesus was less powerful or less endued with the Holy Spirit at that time. The refusal of the townspeople to believe in Him limited the working of His power among them. A church that refuses to trust in God's power to accomplish His plan through them limit what God is going to do. The promise that one can remove mountains according to the prayer of faith seems impossible. Yet Jesus promised that this is possible because it is God's power that moves the mountain (Mk. 11:22-23). The power of God that raised up Jesus from the dead is the power that is available to every Christian, to every church at any moment in time. Paul's own internal longing was to personally know this power (Phil. 3:10).

In his prayer for the Ephesians, his hope is that they would also come to know this power. In that moment, whatever plan God has for His church is not only possible, but actual. The church that taps into this spiritual strength knows something special only reserved for those willing to trust God completely.[6] This is not some Keswick second work of grace. This is simply the realization that seemingly impossible things can be accomplished in the church that connects to God's power by faith. The power of God (Him who is able) works in the church that believes in His power.

---

[6] Peter O'Brien, *The Letter to the Ephesians*, (Grand Rapids: Eerdmans, 1999), p. 267.

God's Power Means God's Glory

The word doxology comes from the Greek word for glory (*doxa*). It conveys the idea of something being worthy of worship or praise. In this case, the connection is between God's power and His glory. He should be glorified because He provides the power that is at work in the church. Specifically, God works through Christ in His church to accomplish His purpose for it. Thus, Paul's statement, "to him be glory in the church and in Christ Jesus" makes sense. God's power in the church is Christ in the church. In the Old Testament, God's glory was linked with His presence.[7] This is called God's Shekinah glory. The Old Testament describes this glory as a cloud (Ex. 34:5); as God's glory (Ex. 16:10), as a cloudy pillar (Nu. 12:5), as the presence of the Lord Ps. (97:5), the glory of Jehovah (1 Kg. 8:11), and as radiance (Hab. 3:4).[8] The New Testament expression of God's glory is expressed in Jesus. John wrote that in Jesus the disciples saw the glory of God (Jn. 1:14, 14:9). The writer of Hebrews revealed the same idea when he wrote that Jesus is "the brightness of the Father's glory, the express image of His person" (Heb. 1:30. Jesus is the glory of God. Wherever He is, there is also the glory of God. Thus, in Christ, God the Father is operating in the church so that both the church and Christ are bringing glory back to Him. This fact is evident in Paul's letters to the early churches in the New Testament.

Rome. The famous salvation text in Romans 3:23 demonstrates that man does not inherently have anything over which he can naturally glory. Every person sins. The result of sin is that it renders us inadequate in comparison to God's glory. Everyone comes short of it (*hystereo*). Without Christ, no one has the ability to reach God's glory (*doxa*). Yet Paul indicates that believers are declared righteous by the grace that God gives in the redemption that is in Jesus (v. 24). The result is that no one can boast that he has saved himself.

---

[7] Ibid, 268.
[8] Matt Slick, "What is the Shekinah Glory of God?" https://carm.org/what-is-the-shekinah-glory-of-god, accessed May 24, 2019.

Corinth. Paul makes this same argument to the Corinthians (1 Cor. 1:26-31). Most of the people in the church were not from important families. They were not considered to be wise or mighty (v. 26). Rather, to the secular world they would seem to be ignorant, feeble, and of low birth (vv. 27-28). In other words, most of the church members in Corinth were not notable. However, because of God's work in them through Christ (v. 30), they were able to humble the wise and the strong. Because of Jesus they were greater than those who were born into nobility. The result of this is that God alone was worthy of glory.[9] No individual, even one who was as spiritually mature as Paul, should boast in himself (v. 29). All the glory belongs to God (v. 31).

The Churches in Gaul. Paul introduces his important letter on Christian liberty through the gospel by indicating to the Galatian believers that they had been delivered from the evil spirit of the age by the God's own will to offer salvation in the sacrifice of Jesus (Gal. 1:4). This statement is so powerful, that Paul interrupts his own writing to add: "To whom be glory for ever and ever" (v. 5).

Ephesus. The entire first section of chapter 1 has a restatement that salvation of sinners is "to the praise of His glory" (Eph. 1:6, 12, 14). Salvation through Jesus is so incredible that God is called "the Father of glory..." (v. 17). It is never by self-righteousness lest any should boast of saving himself (2:9). Everything of value that a Christian possesses is from the riches of God's own glory (3:16).

Philippi. God's glory in salvation is assumed because those who are in Christ are called to be "filled with the fruits of righteousness" (Phil. 1:11). Spiritual fruit in the life of a believer is to God's own glory. Moreover, nothing should ever be done which does not bring glory to God (2:3). Self-glory robs God of what He alone deserves. In fact, what God did for believers through Jesus is amazing. The Lord Jesus poured Himself out for us both in becoming a man (2:7) and in willingly going to His death (2:8). The consequence of this is that Jesus has been exalted by the Father receiving a name above all other names (v. 9). So while Christians are bowing down to Jesus (v. 10), while they are

---

[9] The word translated glory here is not doxa but one that means boasting.

confessing Him to be God's Anointed and the Lord (v. 11a), they are doing it all to the glory of the Father (v. 11b).

Colossae. The believers in Colossae were brought to faith in Jesus through the ministry of Epaphras, someone Paul considered to be a co-worker in the gospel ministry (Col. 1:7). Through his preaching of the gospel, they had come to have hope in heaven, something common among believers (1:5). The result of their testimony was that Paul prayed for them even though he had never been to Colossae. He prayed that they would order their lives in a manner that was worthy of the Lord Jesus (v. 10). This lifestyle was pleasing to the Lord, produced fruit for Him, and was part of how believer's mature in their faith (v. 10). Moreover, Paul prayed that they would gain spiritual strength according to God's own power. He describes this power as "glorious" (v. 11). Moreover, this was attributable to the fact that Jesus was in them. That is the hope of their glory (1:27).

Thessalonica. The Christians in the Thessalonian church were also commanded to order their behavior so as to honor the testimony of God. The reason for this is that God had called these Christians to both His kingdom and His glory (1 Thess. 2:12).

Wherever God is working, through these early churches mentioned in the New Testament, or in a local church today, there His glory is on display because of the power of Christ operating in that church. Anything good, anything of value, anything that is praiseworthy is to God's glory alone. No man, certainly no church, should boast about itself. That is an affront to the gospel and robs God of the glory He is due.

The Doxa Grid

Because the power of God is present in Jesus, Who is in the church, and because this power causes the church to function as it should, the glory for the church belongs to God. Everything that happens under the umbrella of the church should be to God's glory. This is the grid through which every ministry should be evaluated.

Worship

The church must ask itself: Is our worship glorifying to God? In regard to music, it matters less that it is relevant or contemporary or traditional. If it is not glorifying God, then it is not the right kind of music. The vision of John of heaven's worship includes a song that praises Jesus (Rev. 5:9). "Christian music should exalt Jesus Christ, the Lamb of God."[10] Likewise, the preaching must exalt Jesus Christ. The sermon may be interesting. It may be delivered by a charismatic speaker who has no difficulty holding the attention of the congregation. It may be factually correct. It may include textbook explanation of the passage being addressed. It may have pointed application that causes serious personal reflection. If it does not exalt Jesus Christ, that sermon is deficient. The preacher's goal should be to honor Jesus. This is the definition of great preaching.[11] All the other elements of worship should have this as their goal (see chapter 4 for an explanation of the elements of worship).

Church Business

While many Christians agree that worship should be Christ-exalting, that does not always transfer to the more mundane aspects of church life. For example, a congregation that has just been singing about unity and love for one another, has just been listening to a fine sermon on how the gospel applies to relationships between church members, may devolve into a divisive spirit during a business meeting because personal preferences are not being met and because selfishness bubbles up to the surface. Church business should be handled to the glory of God. This includes the way the leaders manage the church's finances. This includes the way the building is cleaned, the grounds maintained.

[10] Milo Thompson, "A New Testament View of the Ministry of Music," JMAT 03:2 (Fall 1999), p. 10.
[11] Bryan Chapell, *Christ-Centered Preaching*, (Grand Rapids: Baker Academic, 2005), KL 594.

Church Ministries

Some churches have Christian schools. Some operate food ministries for the poor. There are hundreds of potential ministries a church can initiate as there are people motivated to serve. Each of these should be regularly reevaluated to ensure that they are focused on God's glory as the goal. Too many church ministries take on a life of their own, the "tail wagging the dog" so to speak. A great example of this can be Christian school athletic programs. Everyone wants to win. What is the point of competing if no one is trying to win? At the same time, God is not glorified where Christ-like love is not being demonstrated (1 Cor. 13:4-5). Sometimes, a hyper-competitiveness overtakes Christian school sports. Every ministry administrated by the church should have the glory of God as its aim.

Amen

Paul concludes his doxology stating the God should be glorified in the church throughout all the ages, another way of saying "forever." There is no time, now or in the future, when the church should not be bringing glory to God. He ends with the word "amen." This final breath is a way of ending something important.[12] It is added here as a way of encouraging everyone in the church to a unified chorus of "so be it." Each believer must come into God's presence with this goal in his heart: "I am coming to bring glory to God." May it ever be that the church's purpose is to glorify God. Amen.

Discipleship Questions

1. Do you think God is glorified more in a larger or smaller church? Does church size determine the extent to which God is glorified or not?

2. What kinds of things limit God's glory in a church?

---

[12] Peter O'Brien, *The Letter to the Ephesians*, (Grand Rapids: Eerdmans, 1999), p. 269.

3. How can church members be reminded to reflect on God's glory every time they gather at church?

4. How is God being glorified in your church?

Chapter 16

Appendix 1: How to Choose a Church

EVERYBODY leaves a church eventually. Even people who grow up in one church and remain their entire lives, eventually leave as they are wheeled out in a casket. Most Christians, however, are part of more than one church in their lifetimes. Pastors are no exception. One recent study puts the median tenure for a pastor at 6 years in one church. That is almost double what it was in the mid 1990s.[1] According to Pew Research Center, the main reason people leave a church (34%) is that they moved. Other reasons cited were things like marriage or divorce (11%), disagreement with church leaders (11%), problems in the church (7%), or a change in personal beliefs (5%). The rest left their churches for unspecified reasons. The most interesting part of the poll is that 49% admitted to looking for a new church.[2]

The Importance of Stability

Leaving a church is not necessarily wrong (and is sometimes the right thing to do), but it always has consequences. First, Christians who leave a church are forced to begin looking for a new one. This process

---

[1] Thom S. Rainer, "Six Reasons Pastoral Tenue May Be Increasing," https://thomrainer.com/2017/03/six-reasons-pastoral-tenure-may-be-increasing/, accessed May 23, 2019.

[2] "Choosing a New Church or House of Worship," https://www.pewforum.org/2016/08/23/choosing-a-new-church-or-house-of-worship/, accessed May 22, 2019.

is arduous and some who leave one church never find another. Second, leaving a church causes a break in the church body. Even if the believer who leaves is not in a visible role like pastor or involved in the music program, his ministry in that church must be replaced by another. This can cause stress on others who remain behind. Third, the natural break in the body of Christ means that some relationships that are forged over many years are broken for good. People who have enjoyed a close friendship find that it is rarely maintained after one or the other leaves the church.

Not Scripturally Anticipated

Going from one church to another is not really something the Scriptures anticipate. This is particularly true for pastors. Relocation was not something that most people did in the ancient world. Moreover, the church was so relatively new that there were very few churches in one particular town. Christians tended to assemble together in one town. Over the centuries, as denominations and doctrinal differences have developed, this has changed so that believers are able to join one church or another. This is not something the Bible specifically addresses.

Leaving Checklist

Before leaving a church, a Christian should go through a checklist of sorts in order to determine if his heart is right before God. Are there any unresolved conflicts? Is there some doctrinal confusion? Will this damage the testimony of Christ in the community? Is this the result of personal pride? At the same time, he needs to be thinking about where he will go next. This means determining God's will for the future. Is this something that is the result of prayer, Bible study, and godly counsel? Are there good alternatives available?

Burning Bridges

The last thing that any Christian should do is destroy the relationships that he has developed in his church by leaving in the wrong way. While he may move on to develop new relationships with believers in a new church, he leaves behind a wake of broken friendships and hurt feelings. There is nothing godly about that.

How to Find a New Church

Before the widespread use of the internet, the only means for finding a church was either by word of mouth or because of an advertisement. Very little could be actually learned about a church before the first visit. Moreover, one visit cannot provide the necessary information needed to assess whether the church is the kind one can join.[3]

The Wrong Research Criteria

Too many Christians make a decision on a church based upon superficial reasons. This may be one of the underlying causes for repeated church shopping. There are good reasons to join a church. Church membership is important. But if one bases his evaluation on the wrong criteria, the outcome is likely to be fraught with problems.

Name. The name of the church is rarely important. Some Baptists have the mistaken notion that all Baptist churches are the same. They refuse to even consider a church that does not have "Baptist" in its name or on the church marquee. The church name is not that important. There are many Bible and Community churches that are biblical and many Baptist churches that are not. Loyalty to God in the Scriptures is more important than the name of a church.

Preferred Translation. Just imagine one of the early Pilgrims wandering into a church in Plymouth and refusing to join because the pastor was not using the Geneva Bible. It is very likely that Jesus used the

---

[3] You may be able to determine that the church is the wrong kind of a church early on, but determining if it is the right church takes real research.

Septuagint (LXX), the translation of the Old Testament into Greek.[4] It seems almost unfathomable that a Christian today would reject to attend a church where Jesus was scheduled to speak because he knew the Lord would not be using his preferred translation. While some are wildly imperfect, all translations are still translations. Because of that, there are always decisions that the translator makes that influence the way the Scripture reads. The best thing would be for every believer to learn Hebrew and Greek, but that is probably impractical. Until that happens, Christians will rely on translators for their Bibles. Choosing to join or reject a church based solely on a preferred translation is not a good reason for doing so.

Particular Hymns or Songwriters. While a sacred atmosphere is crucial in the worship of a holy God, there is nothing sacred about an era of church hymns or a particular songwriter. Every era of church music, which is basically folk music, has its own identifiable musical qualities. Some music styles may be improper for the worship of God, even seriously wrong. But there is nothing special about any one era of church hymnody. Many who visit a church pick up the hymnal (if the church still uses one) and flips through it to see what songs the church sings. This can be helpful information, but is not the main criteria for choosing a church.

Missionaries Supported. Every church has different reasons for supporting missionaries. Some choose to support missionaries based on regions of the world. Other reasons include interdependent relationships between churches (they support the same missionaries); denominational distinctions; particular practices like the same use of one Bible translation (see above); and a personal relationship between a pastor and a missionary. It is good to know what missionaries are supported by a church. Global evangelism is a very important part of church life (see chapter 13). Just because a church supports a particular missionary does not mean that church is the right one.

---

[4] John Barnett, "What Bible did Jesus Use?" https://www.christianity.com/jesus/birth-of-jesus/genealogy-and-jewish-heritage/what-bible-did-jesus-use.html, accessed May 22, 2019.

The Right Research Criteria

Choosing the right church requires serious research and prayer. In order to do this well, the correct priorities should be established in order to discern God's leading to a particular church. These criteria have priority over other things like location and personal preferences.

Church Distinctives. While a church may not be named "Baptist," the distinctives are a good way of measuring if a church is worthy of membership. The questions that Christians should be asking are:

- Is the Bible given priority in this church?

- Is this church filled with believers?

- Is the pastor spiritually shepherding the people?

- Are the members engaged in worshipping God?

- Is the leadership qualified?

Gathering. Another means by which a church can be evaluated is whether or not the
congregation gathers together. If the church is really just a collection of small groups, then the larger church is really not the church, the small group is. At that point, it should be determined if the small group is measuring up to the other criteria. The church's pastor(s) should also be the one preaching most Sunday services. If the pastor is only visible on a screen because he is in a different location, then the church may be gathering together, but the pastor is not among them.

Worship. An entire set of criteria is determining if the elements of worship are being observed. If a church does not baptize new converts or does not emphasize prayer and Scripture reading, then it is not the right kind of church.

Sacred Atmosphere. The spirit of the church should be one of reverence to God. There should not be a flippant attitude where church leaders speak to God or talk about Him as if He was just another "guy."

Church should be serious. There is nothing wrong with humor and every time people gather, something humorous is bound to happen, but it should be spontaneous, not planned. The church is not a comedy act.

Right Leadership. The church should have pastor(s) and deacon(s). This does not mean that the polity requires the pastor to be part of a larger elder board or that there can be no elder board. The biblical standard is congregational rule with pastoral leadership. Deacons should be involved in implementing the pastor's leadership agenda while keeping true to the congregation. Leaders should not bully the people. They should not be cowed by them either.

Serving Saints. A church is a place where disciples of Jesus can actively serve Him. If a church is controlled by one family, or if only a small percentage of people are doing all of the work, this situation is unhealthy. One of the best questions to ask is this: can I see myself serving here?

Discipleship. A church is also supposed to be a place of spiritual growth. Regardless of the church's political structure, it should encourage spiritual growth among its members. This is mainly accomplished through discipleship. There should be opportunities to link up with other members for prayer and Bible study.

Community Engagement. The church should have a good reputation in the community. That reputation should be that the church is where the gospel is preached and where lives are being changed to be more like Jesus Christ. This is only accomplished by the church getting into its community and sharing its beliefs with others.

World Evangelism. The church must have a plan to fulfill the last command of Jesus. Missions should be emphasized in the church. There should be visible evidence of this. There should also be regularly scheduled opportunities to give, pray, and experience missions first hand. If the church is not trying to reach the world with the gospel, it is really not the right kind of church.

Get Involved

Once the right church is determined, do not arrive late, sit in the back row, and then leave the first opportunity available. Get involved. This is what God called Christians to do in this dispensation. The local church is a blessing to believers. Do not allow emotional pain from a previous church to prevent you from being a part of the new local body of Christ.

Chapter 17

Appendix 2: The Heart of True Worship

A large portion of the Bible addresses the subject of worship. The Old Testament addresses worship. In the days before the Great Flood, the period called the "antediluvian era," there are hints in Moses' text that as the world was growing increasingly corrupt, it was also becoming less worshipful toward God. Immediately after the Flood, the descendants of Noah's family built an enormous ziggurat as part of their false worship (Gen. 11:4). Jewish legend teaches that Abraham's father Terah was an idol-maker.[1] His calling to leave Ur and settle in a new land is part of God separating for Himself people who would worship only Him. The generations after Abraham, particularly Isaac and Jacob, continued the monotheistic worship of God.[2] Later, the covenant God made with Israel (Jacob's offspring) was based on their worshipping only Jehovah. This covenant was renewed at Sinai after Israel exited the land of Egypt under Moses. His successor, Joshua, reiterated the worship of God in his famous speech to the people prior to his death (Josh. 24:15).

Unfortunately, the people did not worship God as they should. The

---

[1] There is a cute story of Abraham smashing his father's idol shop while his dad was away from the store. When asked about it, he blamed the largest idol of smashing all the others. His father knew that Abraham was lying because he knew that they were not truly alive as the people believed. But what was he to do? To call Abraham a liar would undermine his belief in the false gods? To believe Abraham would be to admit that the largest idol smashed the others, something he knew could not possibly be true. See Rabbi Robert Barr, https://www.ourjewishcommunity.org/learn/midrashim-legends/abraham-and-the-idols/, accessed March 19, 2019, 3:46pm.

[2] Monotheism: monoà one and theismà god—one god.

book Judges/Ruth reveal that the generations after Joshua went after their own way. God sent judges to rescue the people from oppression and to call them back to worship Jehovah. By the time of Samuel, the people were ready to completely throw off God's rule over them. They required a king just like the nations around them (1 Sam. 8:7). The record of the kings is little better than that of the judges.[3] The middle portion of the Old Testament contains a large hymnal called Psalms. Many of these were written by the "man after God's own heart," David the king. He was the shepherd/king of Israel who wrote many poems of praise to the Lord.

The ministry of the prophets was to call people back to covenant relationship with God mainly by a return to true worship. Elijah, for example, has to repair the altar of God on Mt. Carmel (1 Ki. 18:30). Isaiah cries out for God's people to return to Him. Jeremiah also cries out, but he actually watches the people slide farther away from the Lord. By the time of Ezekiel and Daniel, the nation is too far gone to return. God sends them into exile as He promised through his prophet Moses (Deut. 28).

The exile nearly destroyed Israel as a people. The Northern kingdom, the ten tribes that followed Jeroboam, were decimated by the Assyrians in 722 B.C. They never fully recovered politically after that. The Southern kingdom, the two tribes of Judah and Benjamin, were conquered by Babylon and later Persia (who conquered Babylon). They were allowed to return in stages under Zerubbabel and Ezra, and they rebuilt the walls of Jerusalem under Nehemiah. They rebuilt the temple and were able to maintain some semblance of self-governance, even under the rule of Rome. In 70 A.D., Jerusalem was destroyed by Titus and the people scattered (diaspora). During this time, the people maintained their worship of Jehovah, even if it was imperfect.

---

[3] There were some very good kings like David, Uzziah, Hezekiah, Josiah, and Azariah. There were a few pretty good kings like Asa, Jehoshaphat, Jotham, Amaziah, and maybe even Jehu. In Judah, the rule of the good kings outnumber the bad kings approximately 240 years to 130 years. In the Northern Kingdom (sometimes called Ephraim), there are only 25 good years (depending on your view of Jehu). From the time of Jeroboam 1 to the fall of Samaria is some 180 years of wicked kings. One of the major sins of the people during this time was idol/false worship.

The New Testament also deals with worship. The four Gospels focus worship on the true King, Jesus Christ. Everything about the ministry of Jesus leads people to fall down before Him in praise. The book of Acts, the history of the early church, shows God's people worshipping Him as they come to know Jesus as Savior. The epistles explain how to orderly organize the worship of God in the Church. The Apostle Paul addresses worship in Romans (chapter 12 for example) and 1 Corinthians (chapters 12-14), and the pastoral epistles (1 & 2 Timothy and Titus). Colossians provides a warning against human philosophies that rob God of true worship. The general epistles also deal with worship. John's epistles, for example, are concerned with false worship by the early gnostic heretics and other idolaters. The early churches in Revelation 2-3 are challenged to worship God righteously. Really, the whole Bible, from cover to cover, addresses the important subject of worship.

The Heart of Worship

In the doctrine of worship, a key text is the Jewish *Shema* in Deuteronomy 6. The context of this portion of Scripture is the restatement of God's moral law, the Ten Commandments. Scholars generally agree that the commandments can be divided into two sections, man's relationship with God and man's relationship with his fellow man. Where this division should fall is one of debate, but it is generally agreed it is somewhere between the third and fifth command according to the Protestant reckoning of the Commandments. Moreover, it is likely that the early commands create a kind of foundation from which the rest of the commands arise. The result is the conclusion that when man's covenant relationship with God is right, then his relationship with others will be right also. This means that the entire moral code has its genesis in the first words, "I am the Lord your God...you will have no other gods before Me" (Deut. 5:6-7). The later prohibitions such as those against murder and adultery only have any value as they are understood within the greater context that they are kept as part of one's covenant with Jehovah as the only God. As the Creator, He sets the boundaries for human behavior and interaction with one another.

The Shema identifies this as the most important idea because it calls Israel to acknowledge that there is only one God, Jehovah. In fact, there is an attached promise to this agreement that faithful worship of God will result in a prolonged life (Deut. 6:2) and in the blessings of the Land of Promise (v. 3). Moses later stipulates, however, in the Palestinian Covenant that unfaithfulness to the true worship of God will result in a series of increasingly horrific curses culminating in decimation and exile from the land (Deut. 28:64). These curses are so severe that Moses commands the people to teach the laws of God to their children at all times and in every circumstance of life (Deut. 6:7-9). The danger, Moses argues, is that the Israelites would forget God (v. 12) resulting in idolatry (v. 14). This is, in fact, what ultimately occurred.

The Shema defines worship as love (*'ahab*) for God with one's whole self. This includes the important aspects of one's being; his heart (*leb*), his soul (*nephesh*), and his force or abundance (*ma'od*). Stripped down, worship is a fundamental desire for God. This kind of passion is what David expresses when he compares his desire for God to a thirsty deer panting for water (Ps. 42:1). Worship is "a direct expression of our ultimate purpose for living...."[4] This love is central to keeping the covenant commands (Deut. 5:10). As Puritan Thomas Watson observes, love is the summation of the Moral Law. It is "the soul of religion and that which constitutes a real Christian."[5] Meditating on the commands involving man's relationship to other men, the Apostle Paul noted that love is the fulfillment of the law (Rom. 13:8, 10). Commands such as "do not commit adultery" and "do not murder" are summarized in the command to love others as one loves himself (v. 9). Likewise, commands towards God such as faithfulness to worship Him alone finds its theological center in one's love for God. God-lovers do not set Him aside in order to worship other gods. They do not attempt to reduce Him to a being such as He created—a bird, a beast, a serpent,

---

[4] Grudem, Wayne, *Systematic Theology*, 1004.
[5] Watson, Thomas, *The Ten Commandments*, 6.

or even a human being (Rom. 1:23). No one who truly loves God will be guilty of treating His name as nothing. Love is truly the summation of the law.

It is also complete. The Hebrew (*kol*) translated "all" augments each of the terms so as to be a total commitment of one's life. The entirety of one's heart should be to love God. Every aspect of one's soul and strength must be focused upon Him. Watson enumerates six ways in which we should love God; sincerely, personally, mightily, affectionately, superlatively, and constantly.[6]

Heart. In Hebrew, the heart is not the seat of the emotions. "The heart is, in Old Testament anthropology, the seat of the intellect, equivalent to the mind or rational part of humankind."[7] Ancient Jews would not be able to comprehend the use of a red heart to symbolize emotional love on Valentine's day. Their heart was the inward man, the literal thinking process of an individual.

Soul. The soul is the immaterial part of man, just as real and alive as his physical body. "In its most basic sense, the Hebrew word, *nephesh*, means 'life.'"[8] It is the personhood of an individual. It is "the center of various spiritual and emotional experiences of mankind."[9] It is the "person qua person."[10] Without a soul, man is simply an animal. A soul-less human is a body without the personhood that makes man unique among all of God's creation.

Might. The strength of man is his ability or force to accomplish something. This involves man's physical abilities. In Matthew's rendition of this verse, "mind" is used instead of "might." Mark and Luke both use the word strength, even though their Greek word (*ischus*) differs from the Septuagint term (*dynamis*).[11]

Because the various New Testament renditions of this verse are different, it is likely that the way God intends for people to interpret Moses' argument is not to nit-pick the individual terms, but to see that

---

[6] Watson, Thomas, *The Ten Commandment*, 7.
[7] Merrill, Eugene, Deuteronomy, *The New American Commentary*, 164.
[8] Ryrie, Charles, *Basic Theology*, 196.
[9] Ryrie, Charles, *Basic Theology*, 197.
[10] Merrill, Eugene, Deuteronomy, *The New American Commentary*, 164.
[11] Merrill, Eugene, Deuteronomy, *The New American Commentary*, 165.

the whole of man is to love God. "In any event, all three citations of the Shema agree in demanding that one love God with all his being."[12] Worship is, therefore, the whole of one's being set upon love for God alone. In any situation where this love is incomplete or where God is not the object of this love, worship does not exist (at least not worship as God intended it to be).

Sweeping Concepts of True Worship

While the emphasis on worship involves the whole of oneself, there are specific concepts involved. Once again, these should not be divided into orthopraxical segments such as preaching or prayer. Rather, these elements are all contained in any cultic display of worship. These elements are singularity, fear, and obedient service.

Singularity. Just as "the foundation of all truth is that God is,"[13] Christian worship can only be accomplished if God alone is being worshipped. This singularity is fundamental to the Shema. The call of Moses is for Israel to listen (*shama*) to this truth. "Jehovah our God is one Jehovah" (Deut. 6:4). This is a clarion call against the polytheism of the pagan nations around Israel. The Egyptians and Canaanites worshipped many different gods attached to the seasons, lunar objects, and their agrarian economies very much like modern Hindus. In Egypt, for example, there was Nun, the primeval god, along with Ra, the god of the sun. Isis was the goddess of magic. They even worshipped cats (Basket/Sekhmet) among others.[14] The Jews were called to be monotheists. They were not to have any other gods (Deut. 5:7). This is essentially the point of Elijah's sermon at Carmel. "If Ba'al is a god, then you should follow him (1 Ki. 18:21). Israel was caught up by the influence of Jezebel, daughter of a priest of Ba'al from Phoenicia.

---

[12] Merrill, Eugene, Deuteronomy, *The New American Commentary,* 166.

[13] Draper, James, "The Ground of All Truth," Faith and Mission Journal, Spring 1998, 53.

[14] Mandal, Dattatreya, 15 Major Ancient Egyptian Gods and Goddesses You Should Know About, https://www.realmofhistory.com/2018/01/16/15-ancient-egyptian-gods-goddesses-facts/, accessed January 25, 2019, 3:20pm.

The multiplicity of gods was part of the pagan religious landscape. Elijah chided Israel against their polytheistic practices. Later, this problem with polytheism is what resulted in their expulsion from the land. The Jewish diaspora which began under the Assyrian king Sennacherib, and was finalized in the three separate assaults on Jerusalem by the Babylonian king Nebuchadnezzar was a direct result in the people's unfaithfulness to the singular worship of Jehovah. The ministry of the prophets was to call the people back to covenant faithfulness. Because of their unwillingness to do so, the kingdom was decimated, the temple ultimately burned to the ground, and the wall smashed to pieces. This was all according to Moses' own prophecy (Deut. 29:25-26).

Fear. While the word fear (*yare'*) does not appear anywhere in the Moral Law, the entire scene created an environment that would elicit fear from the Israelites at Sinai. God spoke to Israel from the mount shrouded in fire and smoke (Deut. 5:22). The impression on the Jews was so powerful that they believed that to hear the voice of God anymore would result in their deaths (v. 25). This fear is exactly what God desired. He knew that if they feared Him, just the same as if they loved Him, that they would obey Him. If there is one verse which encapsulates what God desired of His people, it is v. 29. God wanted the people to have a heart of fear towards Him so that they would keep His commandments. This is restated in 6:2, 13. Fear is an important element in worship. Perhaps the question is offered: why should God's people fear Him? Moses answers that question in v. 15. God is jealous that we should worship Him alone. God's anger is kindled against those who refuse to worship Him. How terrible that is! Such a sin should result in one being destroyed from off the face of the earth. The verb fear (5:29, 6:2) is in the Qal stem indicating not just the emotion of fear, i.e. to be frightened, but also an awe and reverence that garners respect and honor. This is the kind of fear that C.S. Lewis captures in *The Lion, the Witch, and the Wardrobe* as Mr. Beaver is explaining to Susan the nature of Aslan. Susan asks: "Is he quite safe?" "Safe?" Mr. Beaver replies. "Who said anything about safe? 'Course he isn't safe.

But he's good."[15] It is not worship if there is no fear of God and includes some measure of emotional fear along with reverential awe and honor.

Obedient Service. Finally, a right fear of God is combined with obedient service to God. God's desire (5:29) is that His people would fear Him in order that they might always keep His commands. The Shema also connects fear and obedience (6:2, 12-13, 24). Moses uses three different words to describe obedience. The Israelites were to keep God's commands (v. 2). The word keep (*shamar*) means to guard or give heed. There is a sense in which the people should fear losing the commands of God by not faithfully guarding them. They were also to serve God. The word serve (*'abad*) means to work or labor. Their entire worship structure involved faithful service to God in keeping the cultic covenant practices including the entire sacrificial system. Finally, they were to do the commands of God. The word do (*'asah*) means to act in such a way as to produce something; to make or accomplish something. When Saul failed to slaughter the Amalekites according to God's command (1 Sam. 15:3), Samuel explained clearly to Saul that the machinations of worship, in his case this involved the sacrificial system, were not as important as obedient service (v. 22). To obey is to worship. There is no worship if there is not obedience to God undergirding it. The New Testament uses the word service (*latreuo*) in terms of Christian worship. The very act of presenting our bodies to God as one would present a sacrifice in the Old Testament dispensation is an act of worship because it is service to God.

How to Recognize True Worship

Application

Applying these three elements of singularity, fear, and obedient service encapsulate the means by which true worship may be recognized. While there is still an element of subjectivity, at least in regard to others, one may properly judge his own motives by these standards. The

---

[15] Lewis, C.S. https://www.goodreads.com/quotes/344456-aslan-is-a-lion--the-lion-the-great-lion-ooh, accessed March 19, 2019, 4:32pm.

probing self-evaluation can help determine one's own worship to God by answering these questions: (1) Is my worship to God alone or am I focused on something or someone other than God? (2) Do I have a proper fear of God so that I am not casually approaching Him as if He is an earthly grandfather (old man upstairs) or an acquaintance or neighbor (friend)? (3) Am I serving God with my whole heart? Do I authentically love Him? Is my life committed to doing His will?

Worship is often viewed through its individual visible parts. A church may have a worship leader. The ushers pass the offering plates as we "worship God with our tithes and offerings" (as the phrase has been repeated in churches across the United States). Maybe a deacon stands up in the pulpit to lead the congregation in corporate prayer. In most churches, the pastor preaches as part of the normal worship service. When anything happens that deviates from the expected norm such as a guitar being used in the music portion of the service or the offering plate being replaced by box fixed to the back wall of the sanctuary, if pews are replaced by chairs, then some cry that the church has fallen into practices of *deviant* worship. While that may be true for other reasons; a well-pewed sanctuary (usually in very dark colors like burgundy or blue unless the church happened to be built in the 1970's); the traditional sounds of piano and organ along with a choir singing songs only published by one specific music company; and a pastor preaching from a particular Bible translation no later than the beginning of the American Revolution; and well-dressed ushers passing gold or silver-toned offering plates; while these may be part of an authentic worship experience, there is no possible way to tell solely by these things. True worship must be judged by its singular focus on God, its reverent awe of Him (and possibly even real fright), and its obedient service to Him.

Chapter 18

Appendix 3: The Ordination of Pastors

Jesus is the "head" of the Church, the sole authority in every local church (see chapter 6). He is the vine and we are the branches (Jn. 15:5). There is no human being who holds a special place between the Vine and the rest of the branches. There is no special Branch, unless one is using that in reference to Jesus as in Zechariah 3:8 and 6:12. Baptists have long held that there is no pope and that no human being can claim papal authority. At the same time, individuals are given special authority in the local church to represent Jesus to the congregation. These men are given their authority by God and that authority is recognized in ordination (1 Tim. 4:14).

Conferred Authority

In the Old Testament, there are examples of individuals being ordained to leadership. Aaron and his sons were ordained by Moses to leadership in Israel (Ex. 29:9, 29, 35, Lev. 16:32, Num. 3:3).[1] By this these men were commended to the nation as leaders.[2] Their ordination transferred authority to them by the one ordaining them. In this case, Moses was transferring authority to these priests. The Old Testament also contains examples of people who tried to claim the authority

---

[1] Richard Mayhue, "Ordination to Pastoral Ministry," in *Pastoral Ministry*, ed. by John MacArthur, (Nashville: Thomas Nelson, 2005), p. 108.

[2] Ibid, p. 109.

of the priests for themselves. Korah and his Levitcal delegation were condemned by God for trying to usurp Moses' authority (Num. 16:29-31). Other men such as King Saul (1 Sam. 13) and King Uzziah (2 Chron. 26) were judged for taking priestly authority onto themselves. Uzzah, the possibly well-meaning, but clearly disobedient man was judged by God for taking priestly authority to himself by touching the Ark of the Covenant (2 Sam. 6:6).

New Testament ordination follows the same track of conferring authority on an individual to be a spiritual leader in a church. Peter's address to the disciples in Acts 1 argued in favor of selecting one of the men who accompanied them in their following of Jesus to take Judas' place among the Twelve (Acts 1:22).[3] After it was determined that Matthias should be the man selected to replace Judas, "he was numbered with the eleven apostles" (v. 26).[4] The biblical basis of ordination is that spiritual authority should be conferred onto an individual. Thus, he is different from an Old Testament prophet whose authority was derived from his direct calling from God (Isa. 1:1, Jer. 1:5-7, Ez. 2:3-4, Jon. 1:1-2, 3:1-2).[5] Pastoral ministry is also different from that of the apostles. They were those who had first-hand experience with Jesus. They were sent out by Him (*apostolos*) to be a witness to His life, death, and resurrection (Acts 1:22). Modern day "apostles" are either ignorant or charlatans, neither of which is very good.

---

[3] The means for discerning God's will for ordaining a new apostle was casting lots. There are no other examples in the New Testament of this being employed. Custer notes that it was because the Holy Spirit had not yet come at Pentecost. After Pentecost, there was no need for such an action. See Stewart Custer, *Witness to Christ: A Commentary on Acts*, (Greenville, SC: Bob Jones University Press, 2000), p. 14.

[4] F.F. Bruce cites Eusebius as stating that Matthias was one of the seventy sent out by Jesus in Luke 10 (*Ecclesiastical History i.12, ii. 1*). He notes that Eusebius may not be correct. He also states that Church tradition has Matthias as doing missionary work in Africa. "The Book of Acts," *The New International Commentary on the New Testament*, (Grand Rapids: Eerdmans, 1975), p. 51.

[5] Too many pastors think of themselves as "called" by God directly in the same way as the Old Testament prophet. This makes them, in their minds, to be unaccountable to anyone but God. This is not how the New Testament describes pastoral ministry at all.

Pastoral Authority

Pastoral authority is important. It is unfortunate that many pastors either timidly shy away from their God-given authority in the church (see Paul's counsel to Timothy in 1 Tim. 4:12) or they abuse that authority by establishing themselves as spiritual dictators (see John's remarks on Diotrephes in 3 Jn. 9).

Exercise of Authority. The pastor is authorized by God to teach Bible doctrine to the congregation (1 Tim. 1:3), to lead the church in prayer (2:1), to lead in appointing new pastors and deacons (3:15, Tit. 1:5), to publicly denounce false teaching (4:7), to oversee the membership (5:9, 11), to evangelize the unsaved (2 Tim. 1:8), and to preach the word of God (4:2). Others may do these things or participate in them, but the pastor is given specific authority over these things in the church.

Moreover, once pastoral authority is conferred upon a man, he should be given the benefit of the doubt (1 Tim. 5:19). Many situations arise that put pastors in difficult situations. There are often legal considerations that prevent him from revealing publicly every detail in a situation. His pastoral authority should recognized so that he is protected against slanderous charges.

Limitations of Authority. That does not mean that pastors are free to do whatever they want in a church. They are not the "king" and their wife is not the "queen" of the congregation. Some churches refer to the pastor's wife as the "first lady." This is not a biblical position to take.

Pastoral authority is limited in various ways. First, it is limited in that pastors lead but do not rule the congregation. Congregational rule is an important biblical distinctive.[6] The apostle Peter warned pastors to be careful to "feed" God's flock, but not "lord" over it (1 Pet. 5:2-3). Second, pastoral authority is also limited to the church in which the authority is conferred. There is no authority outside the local church that

---

[6] Larry Oats writes that there are three specific evidences of congregational rule in the New Testament. First, the congregation was the final arbiter of disputes (Matt. 18:15-17). Second, the church appoints pastors and deacons (Acts 6:2-3). Third, congregation chooses members (Acts 15:1-4, 12, 22-23, 30-31). This is taken from unpublished classroom notes: *Ecclesiology* by Larry Oats, Maranatha Baptist Seminary.

allows for a pastor of one church to attempt to exercise authority in another church. This kind of "apostolic" authority usurps congregational rule as the congregation in the other church has not conferred authority onto this man. Third, pastoral authority is limited to the length of time the pastor serves the church as the pastor. He does not retain authority when he changes pastoral ministry or retires. In this sense, ordination is always localized to the individual church which confers authority onto the pastor. It is not "once ordained, always ordained." There are thousands of formerly ordained men who are just laypeople in the church today. These men do not retain the authority of a pastor even if they have acquired wisdom from their previous experience. Fourth, pastoral authority is not conferred on leaders of parachurch ministries. For example, the president of a Bible college is not a pastor (unless he also leads a church) and does not have pastoral authority. He may be wise and skilled in preaching, but he does not have the same authority in his church that the pastor has. Finally, pastoral authority does not give the pastor the right to overrule parental authority in the home. God gives parents certain rights and responsibilities that are not superseded by the pastor. If the situation involves the church, then the pastor may choose to exercise his authority. However, if the situation involves a decision in the home, then the pastor's authority is limited as to what he can do. Just because the family are church members does not give him the liberty to overrule parental authority.

Abuses of Authority. There are hundreds of heart-rending illustrations of pastors abusing their authority in the local church. These are the cases that receive the most attention because the information is so sensational. Not every example of pastor abuse is documented however. Pastoral abuse can include things like:

· Using his authority to abuse someone sexually;

· Using his authority to obtain information that is private;

· Using his authority to overrule the congregation on business matters;

· Misusing Scripture to defend boorish and rude behavior;

· Misusing Scripture to defend unbiblical behavior

Pastors who abuse their authority should be confronted (1 Tim. 5:19). If it can be demonstrated that he has abused his authority, he should be publicly rebuked (v. 20).[7]

Surrender of Authority. Once a pastor is ordained by a church and pastoral authority is conferred upon him by the laying on of hands, he has certain rights in that church to exercise his authority as he needs to. Once he leaves that church, for whatever reason, his authority ends. Unless authority is conferred upon him by another church, he no longer maintains any pastoral authority. At this point, the best practice is for the pastor to surrender his ordination to the church.[8]

The Process of Ordination

While the need for pastors has never been greater, it is foolish to quickly ordain someone to a ministry as serious as is pastoral leadership. Paul specifically warned Timothy about doing this (1 Tim. 5:22). It is difficult to imagine, but some of the men Timothy ordained to ministry caused him great trouble in the church in Ephesus (Acts 20:29). Perhaps some of those were hasty ordinations. Whatever the case, before someone is ordained, he should go through a lengthy evaluation to determine if he is fit for pastoral ministry. It may be that this can be done in three specific phases.

---

[7] I do not know of any examples of a pastor who has been publicly rebuked before his congregation where he has remained as the pastor. There are examples of pastors resigning in disgrace and then returning to apologize to their congregations. This is different from what Paul envisions in 1 Tim. 5:19-20.

[8] Many churches maintain a "pastor emeritus" status for a former, long-serving pastor. This practice seems to be a nice way to reward the pastor for his faithful service. However, in reality it is not a biblical practice and should not be done. "Pastor emeritus" gives the impression that the former pastor maintains some kind of authority in the church when he does not. Often, these men move away from their congregations in retirement. It is ludicrous to call them "pastor" when they no longer hold any pastoral office. Some may continue to do this out of respect for the individual, but it is not something that is necessary.

Phase 1: Examination of the Candidate's Character

The man setting himself forward to be ordained should be examined to his character in order to determine if he is even fit for pastoral work. He should be blameless. His character should not be impeachable. This includes his relationship with his wife (if he has one) and children (if he has any). He should be a morally upright man training any children to be morally upright. He should be self-disciplined, his behavior given over to the Holy Spirit's control (1 Tim. 3:1-7, Tit. 1:6-9). This includes things as mundane as what he eats and drinks, how he spends his time, his personal finances, and what he does when he is alone. He should exhibit a willingness to teach others the word of God. He should be a good person with a winsome personality. He should show kindness to strangers, patience with unreasonable men, and a willingness to walk away from a fight. In no case should he be considered if he lacks the requisite experience to lead a church.

The best way to examine someone on this personal level is for the whole congregation to get to know him over a period of time. It is unfortunate that the way many churches fill their pastoral needs is through a "pig in a poke" method where the congregation does not know the pastor at all before he candidates.[9] Another way to get to know the pastoral candidate is to have his wife fill out a confidential questionnaire. This should include some very personal information that only a wife knows about her husband. There should also be a financial questionnaire along with background checks into the candidates finances and any past criminal history. It is also advised that personal references should be supplied including a personal friend, a business associate, a ministry friend, and a pastoral reference.

Phase 2: Examination of the Candidate's Ability

Pastors are expected to be able to direct every facet of a church's ministry. Because of this, he must be a gifted, talented, and trained man. Churches should examine the candidate to determine what spiritual

---

[9] A pig in a poke is an English idiom that says essentially, never buy a pig until you have seen it.

gifts he has in his pursuit of pastoral ministry. The things that should be determined are:

· Can he preach?

· Can he lead?

· Can he counsel others?

· Does he pray?

· Does he attempt to lead others to Christ?

Some of these things may be more talents than spiritual gifts. That is not a problem. God gives talents as well as gifts. Some of these things can be honed through education and practice. What the church is looking for is whether or not the man is capable of expounding God's word, if he can administrate the church operation, and if he can develop healthy spiritual relationships with other people.

Phase 3: Examination of the Candidate's Doctrinal Positions

This is what most people think of when they think of a pastor's ordination. Typically, the pastoral candidate creates a doctrinal statement where he explains what he believes about God and the Bible. His theology is examined. This usually takes a few hours and pastors from the area are often invited to sit in on the examination. The questions should not be framed to embarrass the candidate, nor should they create unnecessary controversy.

Confirmation of the Candidate by Godly Men

Once a candidate has demonstrated that he is fit for pastoral ministry, there only remains the question of whether it is God's intention that this man lead this specific ministry. In order to make that determination, the candidate needs to be confirmed by godly men in the church.

This is usually called something like the "Pastoral Search Committee." These men (sometimes women are added to this group which is something the New Testament does not anticipate) form "the presbytery" (*presbyterion*). This group is comprised of any other pastors in the church. When such men are unavailable like when the church is too small to have other pastors, the presbytery can be formed using deacons and other godly men in the congregation. The role of this group is to determine God's will regarding who is to be the pastor of the church (Acts 13:2). They do this using various means. First, they should pray seeking God's leading in the selection process. It may be that the best appearing candidate physically or in experience or training is not what God wants for the church (1 Sam. 16:7). Second, they should look at the resume of the candidate. They should establish guidelines for determining how much training and experience the candidate must have to be considered. Third, this group should get to know the candidate as well as they can. Everything about his life should be examined. While there are no perfect pastors, and sometimes pastoral search committees are overly picky when choosing a pastor, it is a greater problem if men are selected with little to no examination.

At this point, the church should be informed of the selection. The presbytery should share with the congregation what it has learned. They should be able to attest to the candidate's character and qualifications. At this point, the entire congregation should be enjoined to pray for God's leading.

Confirmation. Once this has been accomplished, the committee officially presents the candidate to the church for a vote of the members. Reports should be given regarding how he fared in the three phases of examination. The church, having prayed about the matter, should be set to vote. If a church member has a concern, this should be addressed before the vote.

Installation: Installation of a new pastor is an exciting time for a church. The service is brimming with anticipation of what God is doing in the congregation. There is no biblical order of service, but it seems appropriate that hymns of praise to God be sung, prayers of thanksgiving offered, and the vote of the congregation officially recorded. Perhaps another pastor can bring a charge to the new pastor. At the end of the service, the new pastor should be presented to the church. He should kneel at the front by the pulpit. The presbytery should "lay hands" on him confirming his leadership and conferring authority to him as the pastor. The service should close with the new pastor offering his blessing over the congregation God has ordained him to lead.

Chapter 19

Appendix 4: Is Sunday the Lord's Day?

During the life of Jesus, the Jewish religion had become a highly regulated lifestyle that required strict control over every aspect of life. Many people tried to live like the Pharisees demanded but found it nearly impossible to conform. Law never *produces* righteousness, but the Pharisees tried to accomplish that more than most. The law only reveals where righteousness is lacking.

One of the results of the emphasis on law-keeping was a strict approach to the Sabbath. The most severe groups restricted nearly everything even to the point of attempting to avoid going to the bathroom on the Sabbath. There is a story from the time of the Maccabees that about 1,000 Jews were killed by an invading army because the attack came on the Sabbath and they refused to defend themselves.[1] Jewish airlines El Al does not fly on the Sabbath. A snowstorm in the Northeast United States caused a plane to take off too late to land before Sabbath in Tel Aviv. The plane diverted to Greece in order that observant Jews could avoid violating Sabbath restrictions on travel.[2]

Though not nearly that insistent, some Christians argue that Sunday is the "Christian Sabbath." They restrict their activities on Sunday refusing to enjoy any form of entertainment, do any kind of household work, and even limiting how much effort they put into preparing their food for the day. For these believers, Sunday has simply replaced Saturday as the day God's people should "rest" from their labors. Other

---

[1] Shlomo Brody, https://www.jpost.com/Not-Just-News/Ask-the-Rabbi-May-Jews-fight-wars-and-extinguish-fires-on-Shabbat-476204, accessed on May 30, 2019.

[2] https://onemileatatime.com/el-al-flight-shabbat-violence/, accessed May 30, 2019.

Christians totally reject any Sabbath-keeping as being a part of the Church Age. They argue that there is no Sabbath, not even in principle. While the Early Church gathered together on Sunday in recognition of the resurrection of Jesus, these argue that any day is the same as another.[3]

Many believers are left wondering how they should approach Sunday. Is Sunday "the Lord's Day?" Are there restrictions on what a Christian should, or should not, do on Sunday? Is it okay to work on Sunday?

Common Christian Sabbath Approaches

There are two common approaches to a New Testament Sabbath concept. The first approach is called Seventh-Day Sabbath. Those who follow this approach argue that the seventh-day principle is the center of the Ten Commandments. They quote Exodus 20:8-11 as binding on believers in this dispensation.[4] They argue that this is because of the way Moses presents the command as being rooted in Creation theology "for in six days ...." They also point to the way Jesus refers to the Sabbath as in the present tense "is made for man ..." (Mark 2:27). They argue that the way Jesus operated was to reform the Sabbath-keeping rules so that it conformed more to the way the Old Testament writers were teaching.[5] Seventh-Day Sabbath apologists actually keep the seventh day as their day of worship.

The other approach is actually called the Christian Sabbath. This position argues for a restoration of the Westminster Confession that imposes some restrictions on Sunday practice because the Westminster divines replaced Israel with the Church.[6] Thus, they argue in a very

---

[3] Craig Blomberg, "The Sabbath as Fulfilled in Christ," in *Perspectives on the Sabbath: 4 Views*, ed. by John Donato, (Nashville: B & H Publishing Group, 2011), p. 357.

[4] Skip MacCarty, "The Seventh-Day Sabbath," in *Perspectives on the Sabbath: 4 Views*, ed. by John Donato, (Nashville: B & H Publishing Group, 2011), p. 10.

[5] Ibid. p. 21..

[6] Joseph Pipa, "The Christian Sabbath," in *Perspectives on the Sabbath: 4 Views*, ed. by John Donato, (Nashville: B & H Publishing Group, 2011), p. 119.

similar way to the Seventh-Day proponents but replace Saturday with Sunday, ie. the "Christian" Sabbath.

While neither Seventh-Day or Christian Sabbath theologians argue in favor of the Pharisees, they even argue against them, their position is very similar to that of the Pharisees. No one wants to be on the side of the Pharisees, but what other conclusion can they take? How does Seventh-Day and Christian Sabbath positions really differ from the Pharisaical approaches? All three restrict the activities of people by imposing some reading of Old Testament Law onto their actions, the only difference really being in the actual day being observed, the Seventh-Day followers emphasizing Saturday as the day of rest.

What does a Seventh-Day and Christian Sabbath keeper have in common? They both set aside one day for the worship of God in Christ, something every Christian should agree is important, at least in principle. The difference between these two approaches and those who see Sunday as the Lord's Day, the day of worship, is that these other approaches add the restrictions onto Saturday or Sunday. As noted above, they disallow work. They reject entertainment. They will not vacation or travel on their day. While not as restrictive as the Pharisees, there is something Pharisaical in their approach to the Sabbath concept.

The Pharisees Were Wrong

For those Christians who wish to impose Pharisee-like restrictions on the Sunday (their Sabbath), it is imperative to know that this approach has a fatal flaw. The Pharisees were wrong. They were not wrong to observe the seventh day as the Sabbath. That is obviously set forth in the Old Testament. They were wrong in their understanding of how the Sabbath should be observed.

Jesus is Lord of the Sabbath: Matthew 12

It is evident from the interaction between Jesus and the Pharisees over the disciple's approach to the Sabbath that the Pharisees did not understand the Old Testament. Matthew presents the scene as the narrator, but it should be remembered that he was there on that day. The disciples were hungry while they were out on a walk with Jesus, something that the other Gospel writers do not mention in their version of this story. It was the Sabbath day (12:1). They alleviated their hunger by picking ears of corn and eating them. The Pharisees, along for the walk, noticed what the disciples were doing and called them out for it (v. 2). It is likely that the disciples knew that their corn picking violated the Sabbath rules of the Pharisees. They were "working," a clear violation of the Pharisaical view of Sabbath rules.

Jesus responds to their criticism by pointing to King David's actions recorded in 1 Samuel 21. Jesus notes that when David was hungry, he entered into the tabernacle and ate some of the leftover shewbread (Matt. 12:3-4). At the time, David was fleeing from Saul and was in Nob where there were a company of priests. He asks Abimelech the priest for some bread to eat. Abimelech offers David some of the bread as long as he and his men are ceremonially clean. David and his men eat the bread (1 Sam. 21:6). Jesus notes that this was an unlawful act (Matt. 12:4). This situation creates a problem for the Pharisaical position on the Sabbath. David is their revered king. If they argue that he was wrong, they would be taking the position of Saul and Doeg, David's enemies in the story. If they argue that he was right, then Jesus will ask them to explain the difference between the two situations.

Before they can answer, Jesus poses a second argument from the Law itself. He asks them if they had not read how the priests who were in the temple profaned the Sabbath by their offerings, yet were blameless (v. 5). The Old Testament priests were responsible for certain tasks that would have caused them to violate Pharisaical rules (Num. 28:9-10). If the Davidic argument was not powerful enough, the argument from the priests was overpowering. The priests "profaned" the Sabbath, but were still blameless before God. They were without guilt.

Before the Pharisees could respond to Jesus' arguments, He added another argument that changed the entire line of debate. If the disciple's situation was a bit different from David and the priests, Jesus added that there was One with them who was greater than the temple (v. 6). The Pharisees considered the temple to be greater than any of their Sabbath restrictions. Everything flowed in and through the temple. There was nothing greater to the Pharisees than the temple. Jesus indicated that there was something greater, a person. He points to Himself as greater than the temple.[7] His doctrine is superior to that of the Pharisees. Their understanding of the doctrine of Sabbath-keeping was in direct conflict with Scripture. Jesus said to them: "if you only understood the Old Testament." The Lord quotes Hosea 6:6. "For I desired mercy, and not sacrifice; and the knowledge of God more than burnt offerings." God longs for the hearts of men, not for ritual observance. This was the ultimate problem of the Pharisees mistaken notion of the Sabbath. They kept it ritually without really knowing God. They were following dead rules and not God. This is why they failed to recognize Jesus as the Son of God. In Him, all fulness dwelled. Jesus is, and was, all in all. He was the living human embodiment of the Father. Thus, Jesus was the Master of the Sabbath. Could He not determine its boundaries? In Jesus, everything finds fulfillment. The Pharisees were looking at their own Sabbath-keeping as their rest. Jesus said, "I am your rest."

The Sabbath was Made for Man: Mark 3

Not only is Jesus the Lord of the Sabbath, but the purpose of the Sabbath day was not to restrict people's liberties, but to allow them greater liberty to enjoy their relationship with God by focusing less attention on work and more on rest. Thus, the Sabbath was created *for* man, not man for the Sabbath. This is demonstrated by the way Jesus approaches the Sabbath in healing the man with the withered hand. The Pharisees were in the synagogue watching Jesus to see how He would interact with the injured man (vv. 1-2). Mark places this story as the third in a series of three where Jesus challenges the normal conceptions of the Pharisees in regards to their religious practices. The first involved fasting (2:18-22). The second involved the Sabbath in regards

---

[7] There is this temple-tension throughout Jesus' earthly ministry. He cleanses the temple twice and even points to it being torn down and replaced, though He was referring to His body. This was a charge that the Jewish leaders leveled at Jesus at His trial.

to food preparation (2:23-28). This third involved healing (work) on the Sabbath (3:1-6). Each of these stories focuses on the authority of Jesus (1:22, 27, 2:10). The link between these sections is important as it relates to the Sabbath. Notice that Jesus states that He is the master /owner of the Sabbath (2:28). The same God who created and established the code, is able to explain and interpret what it means. He can even change or abolish it. He is "Lord" of the Sabbath.

The scene presents an opportunity for the Pharisees to learn from Jesus about God. The man with the deformity is presented to Jesus. Think about the story this way. The Creator is presented with His creation that is deformed. The Pharisees do this because they want to accuse Jesus (v. 2). Instead of learning from Him, they have rejected Him. They are the creation rejecting its Creator.

This leads Jesus to ask a reasonable question. "Is it lawful to do good on the Sabbath?" (v. 4). The Pharisees did not answer. They were watching but did not speak. This made Jesus angry (v. 5). He was grieved because of their hard hearts. He asks: "Can good deeds break the law?" This is an important legal question. Notice that Jesus is not asking about moral or ethical implications. He is simply asking about the legalities of the situation. In essence, Jesus is asking: "Should we save someone's life on the Sabbath?" Jesus gets angry because the Pharisees cannot answer the question. Their legalism forbids them from doing good deeds on the Sabbath. By their silence, they are exalting themselves over God. So Jesus heals the man.

The Pharisees respond by seeking to murder Jesus (v. 6). They seek counsel with the Herodians, something they were loath to do. They demonstrate that they do not understand the heart of God. By supposedly protecting the fourth commandment, they show that they do not love people. Because Jesus shows His love, they seek to murder Him, thus choosing to break the sixth commandment.

Jesus is the Fulfillment of the Sabbath Command

The very best way of thinking of the Sabbath is to recognize that this command is fulfilled in Christ. In Jesus, that rest is fulfilled. "We obey the Sabbath commandment of the Decalogue as we spiritually rest in Christ, letting Him bear our heavy burdens, trusting Him for salvation, and committing our lives to Him in service, then remaining faithful in lifelong loyalty to Him rather than committing apostasy."[8] The best way to think of our worship of God is through Christ. In Him, we are actually keeping the Sabbath (fulfilling it) because in Christ we have entered into God's rest. Those who argue for a "day" of rest as opposed to the Person of rest (Jesus) create a dichotomy that the New Testament avoids. Sabbath is important. It is vitally important to New Testament believers. Hebrews 4:1-11 explains the nature of that rest. It is that which Christians have in Christ and that which foreshadows a coming rest in eternity (v. 9). It is not kept holy to the Lord when people order their affairs in the hours preceding Sunday so that they can avoid doing or saying, even thinking about anything "worldly," so that recreation or work can be laid aside for worship. There is nothing wrong with worship. It should supersede these things. But there is not a command to approach the Sabbath as a puritan.[9]

Rather, it is best to understand the Sunday as the Lord's Day. There are some principles of Sabbath that can help shape one's thinking about the Lord's Day, but there is no law governing its use. Christians are not bound by any Sabbatarian code. Instead, Sunday presents the opportunity to celebrate the resurrection of Jesus as the means by which believers have a relationship with God. It is not a Sabbath-lite, restricted day. The Sabbath was fulfilled in Christ.

The Lord's Day

Sunday is the Lord's Day. That has been God's plan for Christians in this dispensation since before the beginning of time. God always intended followers of Jesus to worship Him on Sunday. This is the believer's special day. It has no relation to the Old Testament Sabbatical code, not in theology or practice. Some of the elements may appear to

---

[8] Craig Blomberg, "The Sabbath as Fulfilled in Christ," in *Perspectives on the Sabbath: 4 Views*, ed. by John Donato, (Nashville: B & H Publishing Group, 2011), p. 386.

[9] See the Westminster Confession.

be the same, but they draw on completely different fountains of theology. Just as there were no deacons in the Old Testament, that is an innovation in the church, so the Lord's Day is not the Sabbath.

Established Before the Resurrection. In Luke 24:45, the text states that Jesus opened the disciple's minds so that they would understand the Scriptures. Like someone opening the curtains in a room to let in the sunlight, so Jesus opened the curtains of their minds. The disciples were able to operate under a new way of thinking of the Old Testament. It was a "light-bulb" kind of moment. Their thinking process was altered. Before this occurred, the disciples would have thought differently from how they thought afterward. Their theological conclusions changed. Moreover, this breakthrough was not because of new information. Jesus points to Old Testament statements concerning Himself (v. 44). He walks the disciples through the Torah (law), the Neviim (prophets), and the Ketuvim (writings). The disciples begin to see the Scriptures in light of the life and ministry of Jesus. One of the things that they learn is the significance of the first day (Sunday). The first day was established in the prophetic record. Jesus would rise the "third day," a reference not to Wednesday, but to Sunday. It was the third day after His death (v. 46). This was written in the Scriptures (*graphe*). In other words, God had already codified that Sunday was a significant day before the Saturday command was given. Sunday's significance predates creation. Sunday was always going to be a significant day even if it was not considered to be so in the Old Testament dispensation. This is part of the mystery of the church revealed in the New Testament. God knew which day Jesus would rise from the dead. He set it up that way.

A Dawn of a New Dispensation. Jesus explains that there were new parameters of the new dispensation. Repentance and remission of sins would be preached in the name of Jesus to the nations (v. 47). The localized commission (Luke 9:1, 10:1) was replaced with a global commission. Salvation was always by grace through faith in God. The New Testament sharpens that focus to grace through faith in Jesus (Eph. 2:8-9). The gospel of the kingdom was expanded to explain that Jesus had to suffer on the cross, be buried, and rise from the dead (1 Cor.

15:3-4). There is real Pauline language in Luke's writing (Luke 24:47-48). The focus was on the name of Jesus. This is what Peter and John explain in Acts 3:6 and 4:12. This is what the Pharisees try to quash in 4:18. They hated the name of Jesus.

The disciples were witnesses for Jesus. They would show forth this truth by what they said (the gospel) and by how they lived (Sunday worship) (Luke 24:48). This is what the Holy Spirit would help them perform (v. 49). He was the promise of the Father. He is the Spirit of Christ. The Spirit comes alongside Christians to comfort their hearts in a world that hates believers and to encourage them to live right before God.

The Lord's Day Observed

The two approaches to Sabbath, the Seventh Day Sabbath and the Christian Sabbath, attempt to carry over the Old Testament Law into the New Testament life. In doing so, they bulldoze over God's intent of establishing Sunday as the Lord's Day. Even a Sabbath-lite concept that imposes Sabbath principles does not fully explain what Jesus is initiating in Luke 24:45-48. These approaches also miss the fact that Jesus fulfilled the Sabbath. They pile up some legalistic-like rules onto Sunday worship that takes the teeth out of the Lord's Day.

For those who are confused about this particular issue, the best way to think of it is this way. Focus less on the day and more on Christ. Yes, the day is important. Sunday is the "third day," the day Jesus rose from the dead. But the day is about Jesus. Make your Sunday about him. Take your eyes off of the world and what it is doing on Sundays —sports, recreation, relaxation—and focus your energy on what Jesus is doing. This will turn Sunday from a legalistic requirement into a blessing.